Legends and Tales : of Old Munich :

Told by Franz Trautmann

:: Translated by ::
Amelia Curtis Stahl

:: J. J. Lentner · (Ernst Stahl) ::
Munich :: MDCCCCX

19 o

Kessinger Publishing's Rare Reprints
Thousands of Scarce and Hard-to-Find Books!

We kindly invite you to view our extensive catalog list at:
http://www.kessinger.net

Translator's Note.

———

Changes which have taken place among old landmarks of Munich, since this book was written in 1863, are indicated by the foot-notes, in the preparation of which, the translator owes grateful acknowledgment to the courtesy of Prof. Dr. Karl Trautmann, and Geheimrat Ernst von Destouches.

Munich, January 10. 1910.

Contents.

Concerning the Origin of the City of Munich.

Whereas this book treats of divers legends and tales of Munich, a few words concerning the origin of that city are surely fitting.

And that happened as follows: In ancient times, Emperor Charlemagne drove the Bavarian duke, Tetzel, from the throne, and banished him to a monastery, because he would not submit to Frankish sovereignty, for which one can hardly blame him. Thereupon, dukes from foreign lands came into power, and the last of the same was Duke Heinrich der Löwe, who ruled over both Saxony and Bavaria.

Now Heinrich der Löwe, who had a very sharp eye for his own interests, noticed that it might be of great advantage to him, if a certain bridge, instead of spanning the river at Vöhring, should be brought up a little nearer to that spot where Munich now stands.

While that idea was maturing, the Duke enclosed a sufficient space with ditches and walls, but it was a much smaller expanse than the traces of the city-walls indicate today. He did so, in order to guard himself as securely as possible, for he was not quite easy in his mind in regard to the plan. Thereupon, on a quiet night, or, for that matter, day — the records are not exact on that question — Anno Domini 1156, he fell upon the bridge, destroyed it, and built another, near the aforesaid enclosed space.

By means of that brave and righteous deed he attained the end, that Bishop Otto of Freising, to whom the bridge down by Vöhring had belonged, could no longer levy the duty on salt, but all persons with that or any other ware, were obliged to pass over Heinrich's bridge, and before proceeding further were compelled to pay the Duke the salt-tax. In addition to that came the market-toll, and later the Duke erected a mint.

As may be supposed, all that caused no small rancor and trife; the affair reached the ear of Emperor Friedrich Barbarossa, who decided it in favor of the Duke, two years later. He commanded him, however, to pay over a third of his profits to the Bishop of Freising.

Now that Heinrich der Löwe had proved that he knew what he was about, people moved in ever-increasing numbers, to the place with the bridge, and instead of the few huts, which had stood on the spot which is now upper Kaufingerstrasse, quite a village grew up. He invested it with a court-of-justice of it's own, and later with parochial rights, and thanks to all that, Munich gradually became a regular town.

The successors of the Bishop of Freising, Adelbert and another Otto, tried their best to deprive Munich of it's importance, or to destroy it entirely, but in vain; it prospered more than ever, and flourished straight on, through good or bad times, until in the last century, it was called the "German Rome" because of it's many beautiful churches and pious people.

In such wise, Munich sprang up here, in the middle of the twelfth century.

And now, the neighboring places deserve a word also. At that same time, one hears of Ismaning, Brunnthal, Rammersdorf, Schleisheim, Neuhausen and Hohenschäftlarn; a hundred years earlier of Forstenried, Berg and Kempfenhausen; still earlier, in the tenth century, of Feldmoching, Perlach and Mosach; before that, in the ninth, of Alling, Sendling and Pullach; and still further back in the eighth, of Giesing, Hessellohe, Menzing, Pasing and Bayerbrunn. That is back in very ancient times. But the oldest of all is the celebrated village of Drudring, which dates from the Germanic Pagan age, when the Druids still held their uncanny sway.

I could tell much about all that, and, who knows, I may send an especial work upon the subject, out into the world some day.

The success of the following must decide that.

Münchner Kind.

Distinct among the oldest emblems of Munich, stands out the city seal. In the very beginning, it was a castle gate, with two towers; underneath was a head in a cowl, and over the gate was an eagle, gazing upwards [1]).

Later, changes were made, and today it is the full length figure of a little monk, stretching its arms out right merrily, with an expression half jovial, half devout.

What further particulars there are about this monk, and whether the city of Munich derives it's name from the word monk, are questions, which have caused much argument and vexation among wiseacres. It always ended in each insisting he was right, and

---

1) An example is on Marienplatz 16.

consequently, no one was sure of anything. Be that as it may, the monk suits us of Munich very well, for we, ourselves are as jovial and devout as the most jovial and devout of monks.

There is a legend, however, as old as the hills about the origin of the monk, and it runs thus:

In those days when the Hungarians, or Huns, as they were called back in the tenth century, were invading Bavaria again, burning and destroying everything within reach, especially the monasteries, the monks of Schäftlarn on the left bank of the Isar, upstream, thought that possibly they would escape unhurt, because their monastery was low and pretty well hidden.

But news came that a band of Huns were marching towards them. At that, some took to flight, and hid in that place which is now Munich. Others remained, hoping the danger would pass, but were attacked by the Huns and massacred. When those in hiding heard that, they did not dare go home for a long time, but staid in a hut which they built, until they saw, that the emperor and his men had slain all the Huns. Then they returned to their monastery which they found in ruins, and built up again as well as they could. But they did not give up their possession in our region entirely, and came down the river now and then.

Be all that as it may, it is a fact that the very first huts with oats and corn, stood upon the spot where the High Bridge [1]) now stands in the Thal.

---

1) The High Bridge was half way between the Rath Tower and Isar Gate, near Hochbrückenstrasse.

Consequently some are of the opinion, that because monks tarried on the aforesaid spot, it came to be spoken of as, 'at the monks' and little by little the name München developed.

The Cross in the Wieskapelle[1].

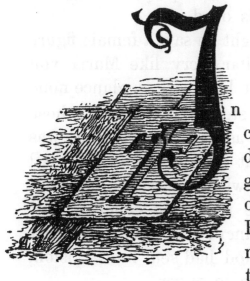

In the walled-up and ancient chapel on the Wieden, Wieskapelle or Herrgottskapelle as it was often called, behind St. Peters, there was formerly a cross graven in the pavement.

Old people used to tell me about it when I was a youngster, but the chapel had long been abandoned even then, and served as a storage place for old documents and the like, as it does today. Some time later, I once had a chance to go in, and I hunted everywhere but did not find anything. Be it, that the carving, which they had told me was even then getting blurred, had now become entirely invisible, or the stone had been turned over, or removed, I was sorry enough not to find it. Whether it comes to light again in the future or not, it was an interesting old relic and the tale about it was as follows:

---

1) A tablet on the east wall of St. Peter shows the spot, where it stood.

Duke Ludwig der Strenge, who, as is well known, caused his wife, the beautiful Maria von Brabant, of whom he was jealous, to be killed, Anno Domini 1256, at Donauwörth, was harassed by ever-increasing remorse, and came often from the royal castle, or when he was abroad for any other reason, to pray in the Wies-kapelle for forgiveness of his deed.

Here, one day, he thought he saw a female figure on the epistle side of the altar, very like Maria von Brabant, who looked over at him with a glance none too mild, but still not too stern, and around whose neck was a red line, as fine as a hair. That last was the surest sign for him, that it was she. He bowed his head in great grief, and when he raised it again, he saw nothing more of the form and concluded, it had been a picture of his fancy; but still, his spirits were somewhat raised, for God had sent him a vision, which had not looked at him in anger.

He gave thanks for that, filled with a still greater longing for forgiveness, and raising his arms to heaven he said with all possible fervor, "Oh Domine, absolve me per innocentiam Mariae". He said that twice, and when he had ended, music gradually became audible, and it was as if angels were singing. It could have been nothing else either, for he knew that beside himself, no one was in the Wieskapelle. So he listened right deferently and when the singing ended, he repeated a third time, what he had said before.

Then he became aware of a sweet voice behind him which said, "Ludovice, te absolvit Dominus noster!" At the mention of God's pardon, he turned around filled with joy, to gaze into the shining countenance of Maria von Brabant, who said further, "Sicut Deus et ego." Which means, "like God I forgive thee", and vanished.

Thereupon Duke Ludwig der Strenge fell upon his face and wept like a child, bitterly, yet full of gladness because he knew then, that he was forgiven.

And, they say, as a memorial of what had happened, he caused a cross to be cut into the stone, where Maria had stood behind him.

The Little Faust Tower[1]) at Sendling Gate.

loft on the city-wall, to the left of Sendling Gate, as one goes out, is a peculiar, little pointed tower with a fist (Faust), which seems to menace far and wide, on it's top.

Some people used to think a court-fool was once walled in there, because he had delivered over the keys of the city to the enemy. They were right in the delivering over, but not in the court-fool, for the tale about it is as follows.

About two hundred and sixty years ago, two dukes, Ernst and Wilhelm, ruled together in Munich.

These two had a wild, restless cousin, by name Ludwig, who gave them much trouble and often; gradually, though he began to behave more peace-

1) The tower was taken down in the beginning of the seventies of the nineteenth century.

fully, letting it be rumored, that most of the time he was unwell, and by those and other means, he succeeded in making his princely cousins feel quite secure.

However, as soon as they were not on the lookout for any evil, he began to plan their entire ruin, intending to drive them wholly out of the city and seize Munich, and he was already discussing the matter with the burgomaster of the place.

The latter, hoping for golden thanks, was treacherous enough to enter into the plot to betray his rightful lords, and when they had come to a final understanding, he began to play his part very cleverly.

He selected a few bad fellows, who in a short time had sown the first seeds of discontent among the people. They carried it farther and farther until the citizens of Munich really thought, they were not so well off as they might be. In short, a wild, rebellious spirit awoke among them, and no one inquired any longer who had provoked it; soon, there was nothing but uproar and riot everywhere.

While all that was happening, the treacherous burgomaster behaved as if he were highly indignant, issued several proclamations of warning, and always quieted things down again, for which reason, the Dukes placed still greater trust in him.

But the uproars and riots always began afresh. Whatever the Dukes did, even if it were for the best, was no longer of any account; here and there, it began to be said they were not even the rightful lords; and at last the taxes were disputed and collected only with the greatest difficulty. Altogether, the prospect was not inviting, for the people were full of suspicion and defiance, and the Dukes, of indignation and impatience, just as the burgomaster had foreseen.

So when the Dukes consulted him as to what was to be done further, he said: "Your Highnesses dislike too great severity, but kindness is out of place here, that is sure and certain. So my sincere advice is this; as soon as any disturbance takes place again, leave this ungrateful city, so that the people may see what it is like when you are not here, and all the money of the princely household flows somewhere else. When they have gone through that experience for a time, you will soon see, they will humbly submit, and implore your return, and never forget the example they have had. But if on the contrary, they still rebel after that, I would not hesitate in your place but would return home, in might and power, and have their vile, obstinate heads cut off by the hangman's sword; a dozen more or less makes no difference!"

He decoyed the kind-hearted Dukes, by that speech into following his advice; at the next disturbance, they mounted their steeds and left the Burg with their whole princely suite, riding across the market-place and past St. Peter, through Sendlinger-gasse to the gate, and out toward Weilheim.

While that was happening, the people stood about in alleys and open squares palavering with each other. The burgomaster, who had escorted the Dukes, to all appearances, humbly, now mounted the city-wall with his accomplices, and stepping to the little, open watch-tower, looked after the departing Dukes from thence, and called out as they disappeared in the distance; "Good riddance, noble lords! We did not do that badly! Shake your fists, if you like! if you attempt anything further, I will shake my fist at you! Huzza! Once outside and you will never get inside again!"

When the Dukes were gone, the palavering went on and on, and grew into mockery; the Dukes, it was said, had fled, because they were afraid, partly of the people, partly of their princely cousin, who was in nowise ailing, but on the contrary, was drawing nearer at that moment to take possession of the city which was his by right.

During all that wild talk, the burgomaster's accomplices played their parts and simulated great fear of the cousin, if he were not allowed to enter the city freely and in peace; in short, the people turned away entirely from their two rightful lords, and looked forward to a golden future, when once the new lord was there.

So when the day was waning, and vespers had been rung, and the princely cousin, Ludwig, was really nearing the city, outside the Anger Gate, with his suite, it was opened wide for him although the burgomaster made a pretense of hesitation.

Thereupon, the new duke entered the city, looking around upon the crowd with a smiling and almost gracious countenance, and a man rode behind him throwing pennies around, as if they were as plenty as blackberries.

At that, one shout of joy followed another, and so it went, until the cousin, now Duke, dismounted at the Burg, taking possession of it, and the people of Munich firmly believed that good times were in store for them.

But they were very much mistaken, especially the burgomaster. For when he went to the Duke the next day and said, "Your Highness, we have won the game!" the latter slapped him on the back and said, "There is no doubt about it, you are quite a man for treason! Only take care and dont try the same with me, for it might turn out badly for you, as I have much better eyes, than my beloved cousins".

Any one can fancy the burgomaster's surprise, fright and disappointment, especially because the princely cousin did not behave in the least as if he had ever mentioned a word about gratitude and a reward of money. He completely ignored the past, on the contrary, and ordered a tremendous tax to be imposed. When the burgomaster stammered that the whole city would rebel at such a demand, he jumped up from his seat, grasped his sword and insisted upon immediate obedience At that, all the burgomaster's good courage forsook him, he was downstairs and in the courtyard before he knew how he got there, and he left the castle grounds, full of humiliation and anger; he went straight to the Rathhaus, when he called together all the citizens and made known what the new lord demanded.

At that, there was a great uproar and each one blamed the other. But strife and quarrelling were of no use, the tax had to be raised, and a week later, the princely cousin imposed another and much larger one.

Things went on like that, from week to week and from moon to moon, and it looked as if the princely cousin would reduce entire Munich to beggary, for his demands were ever larger and more frequent; and when the least sign of rebellion appeared, he sent his soldiers to make short work of it with their swords.

The people were on the verge of despair, for the more prosperous and plucky they had been before, they were just so much the poorer and more discouraged now, and each saw that such a state of things would soon bring them to starvation, because they were reduced to the last penny.

But the burgomaster was not prospering either, for in addition to his anger at the Duke's ingratitude, he was in a sea of trouble over his own accomplices. They were tireless in their demands for reward, and no matter how often or how much he paid them, they always renewed their claims with an increase. They threatened, moreover, again and again, to let the people know who was responsible for all their suffering, and to tell the two dukes, Ernst and Wilhelmus, what he had shouted out after them from the little tower on the city-wall. In case the two lords should return to Munich after all, some day, that would not be a very good thing for him, the burgomaster. So he fell completely into the power of his accomplices and assistants, and after he had given them his all to satisfy them, he was obliged to resort to the money-bags of the city. And above all, they mocked him to such a degree that at last, he lost all control over himself and answered their threats by defying them.

Upon that, the scoundrels lost little time in keeping their word, and slandered the burgomaster in all parts of the town, repeating what he had, to their great astonishment, called out on the city-wall, and that spread like wildfire. Before the day had passed everyone was in a ferment, and in two days more, there was a great riot, the burgomaster's house on the market-place was assaulted, and if he had been there, they would certainly have murdered him. He was not at home, though, but somewhere else not far from the Burg to which he escaped, and implored the Duke for help.

The Duke's contemptuous answer was: "So long as I am here, I will protect you. But when I am gone, you will have to look out for yourself; that may be very soon, for my time is nearly up here. There is nothing more to pilfer from the city, because the people are poorer than poverty itself, and hungrier than church-mice. So all I have still to do, is to plunder the ducal castle and make off with what is valuable. What happens after that is all the same to me. The people have been rightly punished, as I hope you will be. Now you know my mind and you may take that as your reward, you cursed traitor, to break faith with your rightful lords. My charity and leniency are of the first order, for if I wanted to be just, I should have your head cut off!"

When the Duke said that in the presence of his marshal, the burgomaster was badly frightened and tried to stammer something, but the Duke thundered out at him: "Make yourself off! Out of my princely sight!" Thereupon the burgomaster wheeled around to the left and out like a flash; the Duke, however, sent a few soldiers after him. They brought him home and drove the crowd away and guarded his house all night so that no harm came to him.

Meanwhile the Duke caused everything of gold or otherwise of value, that could be found in the castle, to be heaped up in waggons.

That went on all night until daylight, and just as the seven o'clock mass at St. Peter was ended, the Duke flung himself upon his horse in the Burg court-yard and rode off with all his counts, knights and warriors, the soldiers from the burgomaster's house among them. In their midst, were the waggons laden with booty, and in that fashion, they rode through Burggasse, past St. Peter, and through Sendlingergasse toward the city gate.

The people flocked thither, murmuring and reviling, but the Duke took no notice of them except to laugh as if amused at their helpless rage; but at Sendling Gate he stopped, and turning with his horse, he reached into his money-bag and threw a handful of pennies among the crowd, calling out: "There! Take my thanks! See what your hatred and anger are worth to me! You deserve no better! Many greetings to your burgomaster, who has served you this trick, other-wise I never should have gone so far. Sound a blast trumpeters!"

Thereupon he put about, and rode out through the gate, his retinue and the waggons following him, all straight ahead, then to the right toward the Frei-sing highroad.

In that fashion, the princely cousin left the city

of Munich behind him again. The people, however, hurried back to the market-place to revenge themselves upon the burgomaster.

He suspected what was in store for him, and tried to hide here and there, but no one would give him shelter. He turned from one place to another but there was refuge nowhere and everywhere the cry "Away with you, traitor!" Then he fled through the streets and alleys, with the people after him led by his own accomplices, until he gained an open court-yard near Sendling Gate. There he climbed a wall, and found a quiet path, which led to the tower on the left. He slipped in, bolted the gates, and went toward the city-wall, intending if worse should come to worst, to climb or jump down, and gain either free-dom or death thereby. He went up the stairs, in-tending to kill the sentinels, if they should bar him the way, but he thought he was safe for awhile from the rear.

That was not the case, however. The accomplices had discovered his path instantly, the crowd pushed on, the gates were broken in, the accomplices ran up the stairs, followed by as many as could crowd in, and they all shouted to the sentinels "seize the traitor!"

Thereupon the wall-sentries rushed at him from infront and the others from behind, so that the burgo-master did not know which way to turn, and was not able to get any further than the little open tower, from which he had mocked the Dukes. He tried to climb up there and jump over, but did not have time before they had hold of him.

So he pulled out his sword shouting "Not without
paying first!" and slashed and stabbed all around.
When he recognized his assistants and accomplices,
he called out: "You against me, you scoundrels, you
who were my instruments! So you are trying to
whitewash yourselves! Wait a minute and I will
color you red!" And he cut and hacked at them, in
a rage, they returning it. He had better luck, though,
than they, for he killed the first as well as the second,
and he pushed the third over the parapet into the
town below, where he fell with a shattered skull.
then he turned to the others. They shouted and
yelled and struck out at him, and he at them, front
and back. Although he wounded many a man, he did
not escape entirely, himself, and at last he was quite
exhausted, and saw his fate clearly before him. Thereupon he summoned his last strength, calling out:
"You'll never get me alive!" and tried to follow his
accomplice over the parapet, and shatter his own head.
But the others pulled him back and knocked him
down; even then he raged and struggled for a long
time until he was bound and shackled.

Then they led him away, back through the pas-
sage, down the stairs and scaffolding of the tower to
Sendlingergasse, and along through the town to Falken
Tower, where they threw him into the darkest dungeon.

On that same day, the people deliberated with
the town-counsellor, who had been innocent in the
whole affair, and a decision was reached, which pleased them all.

Thereupon, three gentlemen of the council and
six citizens mounted their horses. They rode away

2*

together, to the two rightful lords, who were some where near Dachau.

They confessed everything that had happened and implored forgiveness for the sorely-tried city, "because the people are good", they said, "and of the very best sort; but they were tempted and deceived with a devilish cunning. So if the gracious lords would keep that in mind and not lay it up against them, but return, they would be welcomed with repentance and great rejoicing."

Not two days passed before the Dukes approached, and at vespers, rode around the whole city, to the blast of trumpets, and each gate was opened to them. At last they made a triumphal entry through the Anger Gate, and when they were in the city, they halted a moment and Ernestus said to the people: "A severe and lasting punishment is what you deserve, for you have sinned deeply, and ignored a sacred duty, as if you were better off with someone else than with us, who have always meant well by you! Have you found that out now for yourselves! You deserved it all, our cousin was right, when he said that! But you are pardoned and forgiven, and everything is forgotten. No sign of the misfortune must remain, except that you will have empty purses for a long time yet, although the real loss is ours, and that the Anger Gate [1]), yonder, will be walled up. And that will be a sign for ever!"

The people broke out into shouts of joy at such mild words. The Dukes rode along the Anger, across

---

1) The old Anger Gate was taken down at about the same time with the Faust Tower.

the market-place and so on, to the castle courtyard, where they dismounted. They discovered, then, that the Burg had been emptied of every thing of value, and were not a little angry about it. They then inquired into all the particulars of the affair from the very beginning, and found out the burgomaster's part in it, and above all what he had called out after them.

The next day, the people were summoned to the Rathhaus. The Dukes rode hither also, and stopping at the door commanded, that the burgomaster be taken out of the Falken Tower and brought there.

He came accordingly in chains and fell upon his knees before the Dukes, begging for his life. But all the people cried out against him. At that the Dukes made signs for silence and Wilhelmus, it is said, spoke thus in a loud voice.

"You satanic fellow, you beg for your life? You may have it, but you would have done better to beg for death, I can tell you that, of a truth. For you may live, traitor, but in such a way, that death any day would be more welcome." Upon that he stopped speaking and his brother Ernestus took up the word saying: "Do you remember the advice you gave us, and what you called after us from the little tower, when we were riding away, duped by your cunning? You shook your fist, in mockery at us and called 'you are outside and will never get inside again.' Well! Are we here again or not? Your word has turned out a lie. But the word we give you in return, will remain true forever. And that word is as follows: you will be walled up in that little tower, from which you reviled and insulted us, two bricks' space will be left, through which your scanty fare will be given you, and there you will stay as a counter play to your own word; you will be inside and will never get outside! Just as you, who are to blame for the people's suffering and misery, shook your fist at us, in defiance of justice and duty, even so we shake ours forever at you and every traitor, in a symbol, from the top of your prison! It will carry your disgrace down to posterity. It may serve as a timely warning to him, who used you to drive us away, and lead our faithful people astray, that we intend to revenge ourselves upon him, when the time comes!"

At that the burgomaster broke down in total despair, and the jailers pulled him on to his feet again and took him off to Sendling Gate and up through the passage to the little pointed tower. The masons were already there, the people surged down below on the city side, shouting up curses by the thousand, and before long, the burgomaster was walled in.

That was his reward! And soon after, he heard hammering above him, the fist was being riveted to the little tower.

So that was how the Dukes gained possession of their city again, and the burgomaster came to his narrow jail.

He lived in it four half years, and the wall-sentries heard him raving and raging often enough; then in the course of time, that changed to plaints and sighs, and at last he did not take his food at all, and asked for a priest. The latter came accordingly. He confessed to him and intrusted him "to beg forgiveness of the Dukes and of the whole city, and to implore them to pray a Pater Noster and Ave Maria, out of compassion for him because his time was drawing to a close."

The priest delivered the messages, and many prayed for the soul of the burgomaster.

The next day one heard only a low whispering in the little tower, and the second following day, nothing more at all, which indicated, that he in the little tower had died.

Then they broke into the wall, and found the dead burgomaster. His hands were folded reverently together, and judging from that, he had met his end quietly and bravely.

They carried him out and buried him in the churchyard of Heiligen Geist. That graveyard has been destroyed in the course of time, so one does not know now, where the burgomaster lies.

The little tower, however, remained open for the future, and the fist up on it's point. Even today, it speaks of the disgrace of traitors just as the Dukes said.

And the word of the two Dukes concerning their princely cousin came to pass also.

For later, when he heard that the good people of Munich had made some money again, the desire awoke once more in that wild lord, to seize the city, this time by force as he had before succeeded in doing by cunning. He wanted to pull down that sign of warning, and make the people as poor, as he had done the other time.

Therefore he chose what he thought was the right moment, and marched forward with military forces, but very secretly. The Dukes, however, had noticed his game, called everyone to arms, and marched out against their cousin, meeting him somewhere near Blutenburg, which place received it's name from all the blood which flowed then, and there they fought him and his followers, so furiously and fiercely, that he suffered an ignominious defeat, and so barely escaped with his life, that he did not dream again of any designs against Munich, or of duping the true-hearted people therein.

But heaven punished him still more severely because of his crime against his cousins. For his own son rose up against him, he was taken prisoner by him and led from place to place, stripped of all power and possessions, and at last confined in a tower at Burghausen, where be stayed until his death.

Dragon Corner on the Market-place [1]).

ragon Corner has a particular significance for the city of Munich and the saying about it runs thus:

In Ao. 1464, a dragon bringing the plague, flew in at Schwabing Gate; after soaring here and there, in the air, it descended at last on the corner of the market-place. Then there was a panic, and no one know what to do, until strong Duke Christoph came galloping in from Grünwald castle, and killed the ghastly monster. One can read the whole story from the beginning, when the towerkeeper of St. Peter heard the dragon whizzing through the air, to the end, in my "Abenteuer Herzog Christophs", as well as what old Herr Bart had to do with it, and his wicked housekeeper, and

---

1) Marienplatz was formerly called the market-place.

pious old Monica, to say nothing of the dukes Sigmund and Johannes; the latter came to his death through his love of fighting, for the dragon breathed it's poisonous breath upon him. The book sets forth all that, and much else, clearly and plainly.

The Spoon Landlord behind the Rathhaus.

Even so faithfully does the above-mentioned book tell about the landlord of the spoon, at the little fountain behind St. Peter, next the small staircase of the Rathhaus. In a few words, though, the story is thus.

Once there lived in Munich two men, one of whom was named Achzenit and the other Ruprecht. The first was a wild disorderly fellow, and the second was so miserly, that he scarcely dared eat and drank absolutely nothing but water, while the first revelled in nothing but wine.

The water in the little fountain behind the Rathhaus was very fresh and Ruprecht was wont to take his stand there every day, drinking from a big spoon, and offering water to the passers-by. Therefore the spendthrift Achzenit nicknamed him the 'landlord of the spoon', and to annoy him took up his stand also at the little fountain and drank wine instead of water from a spoon, which he filled continually and offered to the passers-by.

That gave rise to much bad feeling and quarrelling, and while Achzenit mocked at Ruprecht for his stinginess, Ruprecht mocked him in return for his prodigality and prophesied, he would come to the wooden punishment donkey yet. The latter stood on the market-place[1]). And in fact, the prodigal's money began to disappear faster and faster, until at last he possessed nothing but a bit of meadow, and the miser was glad, that his prophesy had come true. But Achzenit was full of cunning and managed to get the report started, that a treasure lay buried in that bit of meadow, by which he tricked the avaricious Ruprecht, and they got into such quarrels about various money loans, digging and not finding anything, that at last, they both had to ride the wooden donkey.

That singularly droll tale was the origin of the ladle[2]) on the little fountain, and took place in the year 1464 or 65.

---

1) An old print of Marienplatz. in the Stadt Museum, shows the punishment donkey standing at the west end.
2) A ladle still hangs there.

The Lion in the Thal[1]).

oubtless the lion —, many think the carving is a lioness — over the door of the old chief-justice house, next the Rathhaus in the Thal, is a genuine and very ancient token. No one knows exactly how it came there, but that it had some reference to the world-renowned Duke Heinrich der Löwe, is almost without question. Probably it was thus:

That same Heinrich, when he was ruling the land of Bavaria, but still as a stranger among us, built a castle, about where the Rathhaus now stands, wherein he lived during his various sojourns in Munich, and over the door, he put his favorite device. Later, Ao. D. 1180, after many disputes with Emperor Friedrich der Rothbart, he was put under ban of the em-

---

1) The old relief is in the Stadt Museum and a copy is on the house no. 2 in the Thal.

pire at Würzburg and Gelnhausen, and lost his duke-
doms of Bavaria and Saxony. In his stead, a prince
of the old house of Wittelsbach came to the throne
again, namely Otto. The aforesaid castle probably
stood as it was for sometime, until the Rathhaus was
built and they tore down the building in question.

To prevent the device from being lost, they very
likely put it up on a wall not far from where it was
at first. And there it is still, a reminder of how the
greatest power can be laid low, to make way in the
world for long-oppressed justice.

The Emperor's Stone in the Cathedral.

particularly interesting memorial of old Munich, is the red marble relief in the monument[1]), which Elector Max I raised to Emperor Ludwig der Bayer.

Formerly, the marble lay in front of the high altar over the crypt. It depicts the good emperor sitting upon the throne, beneath him, stand Duke Ernst and his son Albert, who have just become reconciled, for the sake of their great ancestor. The lion, fawning upon Duke Albert, is clearly symbolical of that. There is no doubt about the reason

1) The mausoleum in front of the big door under the organ loft.

of the quarrel between these two. On the one side, namely, because the father, Ernst, caused his son's beloved Agnes Bernauer to be drowned at Straubing; on the other side because Albert for that reason almost provoked a regular war against his father.

But the relief was also intended to be a word of warning in general to all future princes, and a reminder of the vow they had made to preserve peace among themselves.

In former times when the marble lay in an exposed position, no one left Munich without having seen it, and it was a faithful recorder to all, of sorrow and strife, reconciliation and renewed love, as well as of the renown and glory of the house of Bavaria, which had produced a German and Roman emperor.

The saying, that Emperor Ludwig is buried somewhere in the cathedral, sitting upon a throne and wearing all the imperial insignia, is not true. His bones lie with those of many other Bavarian princes, in the large coffin in the crypt of Unser Frauen, and the reason is this; In the time of Max I, the old coffins were fast falling to pieces, and so he commanded that the bones of his ancestors be collected, each provided with it's name, and laid side by side, and one over the other, in that large coffin.

While we are on the subject of that collection of princely skeletons, it may be fitting to mention the names of those, who are resting in the coffin. There are eleven of them:

Emperor Ludwig, der Bayer.

His wife Beatrix.

Her son Ludwig, der Brandenburger.

Duke Stephan mit der Hafte. (The Hasty.)

Duke Ernst I and his duchess Elizabeth.

Duke Sigmund, the founder of Unser Frauen cathedral.

Duke Albrecht IV or der Weise, and his wife Kunigunde.

Their son Duke Ernst, Bishop of Passau, and then Archbishop of Salzburg.

And Duke Wilhelm IV called der Standhafte (The Steadfast.)

Had they all but small Rest here below,
It will be all the sweeter, the Eternal Peace!

The Black Footprint[1] under the Organ of Unser Frauen.

arious tales exist about that black footprint. One runs thus: The Evil One made a compact with an architect, and promised him money for a church, provided he could see no window in it. So when the Evil One saw a great many windows from the outside, he thought he had won and said to the architect, "Your time is up, so come along with me!" Thereupon the architect answered "No such hurry! Just follow me!" And then he led him to a spot in the church from which all the windows were hidden by pillars.

That same Evil One is supposed to have flown into a passion at such cunning, and to have shrieked horribly and in hurrying away, to have left his footprint behind.

---

[1] Between the Emperor Ludwig monument and the big door.

Now the question is whether to believe that or not; for in such a case the devil must have stood on his good foot and have held his cloven hoof up, the whole time. And even if that were so, why did he leave no traces of either his good foot or cloven hoof, in his rush toward the giant door. He must simply have flown out in his anger and rage. But the whole affair was probably quite different and as follows:

In the year 1468, when the much-renowned, strong Duke Christoph of Bavaria, was living in Grünwald castle, he received news that his brother Sigmund was thinking of building a large cathedral in honor of the Virgin Mary, and exclaimed, "Right he is, my lord brother, but he will have to whistle for the money!" At the word 'right' he stamped on a flat paving-stone, leaving the faint outline of his whole foot, and later they carved the impression deeper into the stone, which in the course of time was placed where it is now, where formerly, the view of the church had it's carefully planned obstructions.

So were the facts and not otherwise. Whoever wishes to know more, will find it in the "Abenteuer Herzogs Christoph".

St. Onuphrius[1]) on the Old Egg-market near the Rathhaus.

Upon this subject, there have been many different opinions; why the picture, which represents a most holy king's son from Asia, was painted here, has caused much research. The surest information, however, is probably the legend as it went among the people, and was as follows:

At about 1490, a man named Heinrich Pirmat lived in Munich, by trade a shopkeeper; he was, moreover, very pious, and would gladly have gone on a pilgrimage to the holy grave at Jerusalem.

But the thought of his housewife hindered him, because she was always ailing, and in addition, was

---

1) Marienplatz 17 has a modern fresco of the saint, as a memorial of the old one which was in that place.

well on in years, and as he did not know how much longer he would have her, he did not want to leave her. But one day in Anno 1493, she departed this life, and as Duke Christoph of Bavaria was just starting with many others, on his pilgrimage to the Holy Land, Pirmat decided to go too, although the undertaking seemed dangerous for him as he was no longer young. He was not so much concerned about himself, as about his brother's little son, whom he wished to bring up like a Christian, so long as God allowed him to live. However he left all that to God's mercy, and made a vow that in case he came back, he would have a large picture of St. Onuphrius painted upon his house. As the picture was really painted, the same Pirmat must have come back safely, and four years later, have kept his vow; or he remained several years in Palestine and who knows what he saw and suffered there. At any rate, the date upon the picture is 1497.

Why he chose Onuphrius from among all the saints, is another uncertain point, but it was either because his nephew was named Onuphri, or in memory of a chapel, which, back in the twelfth century, had stood upon the site of the Pirmat house, and in which the bones of the renowned St. Onuphrius reposed, after Heinrich der Löwe had brought them, with many other sacred relics, back from his pilgrimage to the Holy Land.

Although anyone may see the painted saint, and hear his name mentioned now and then, I have often noticed that the legend of the same, is almost completely unknown.

Therefore I will give it here, as it was told and printed four hundred years ago, in all it's childlike originality:

"St. Onuphrius was a Christian and loved God, and was a monk in the monastery of Mepoligano, and he was raised in a monastery, and there were a hundred other monks in the monastery and they all led a blessed life, and could not speak, except of God or when there was great need of it.

Onuphrius learned the Holy Writ in the monastery from childhood up, and discipline of the spirit; then he often heard the other monks praise the life of the anchorite speaking thus: 'Elias chastised his body in the wilderness and received the greatest virtues of prophesy and of working of miracles; he ascended to paradise in a fiery chariot, and shared the gift of the Holy Ghost with his disciples, and lives still!'

And they said of St. John, the Baptist, that 'he, too, was in the wilderness, and became worthy of baptising Christ'.

And because St. Onuphrius heard it so often, he asked the monks why they praised the anchorite's life perpetually.

Then they said: 'There (in the wilderness) they are much more devout than we, for they live without human help, we do not do likewise for we help each other to serve God, and when we are infirm, we take comfort from one another, and have houses against tempests and much else of comfort, which anchorites have not.

But the angels of God comfort them, and bring them their scanty needs, for God never forgets the poor, as it is written: 'But they that wait upon the Lord shall renew their strength; they shall mount up with wings as eagles; they shall run and not be weary, they shall walk and not faint.'

Onuphrius was much comforted by those words and thought: 'I too will become an anchorite', and pondered a long time. Then he rose one night, secretly, and went his way and carried a piece of bread with him so that he had enough for the fourth day. Then he came to a place and thought, 'here will I stay!'

And he saw a light on one hand, and it was right beautiful. But he was sore afraid, and feared he must therefore return to his monastery. Then a glorious angel walked in the light and spoke: 'Fear not, for I am an angel and have been given thee from thy birth, that I may guard thee, and now I am sent to stay by thee and teach thee the life of the anchorite. Thou shalt live in the work, and guard thy heart zealously. Praise God and do good works, for I will not forsake thee, until I bring thy soul into God's presence.'

After that the angel walked with him six or eight miles to a cave, and it was very beautiful. Onuphrius went up to it, and would see if anyone was there, and called in to it.

Then a holy anchorite came out.

St. Onuphrius fell at his feet and prayed to him.

The holy man raised him up by the hand and gave him the kiss of peace and said: 'Oh my son, come within, thou art my brother in this life and the eternal life!'

And Onuphrius went in to him and tarried long, and the other taught him the life of the anchorite.

After some days had passed, the anchorite spoke to St. Onuphrius and said: 'Arise and go further into the wilderness, there shalt thou too dwell in a cave!'

And the anchorite walked four days long with St. Onuphrius, and on the fifth day, they came to a city, and it was called Calcedonia, and there were palm trees near by.

And the angel spoke again to St. Onuphrius, 'Behold that is thy dwelling, which God has prepared for thee'. And the anchorite stayed thirty days, and taught him how to love God, and commended him to God, and went home again, and came back often to St. Onuphrius, to see if it was well with him.

And one day, the anchorite came again to him, and fell down and died.

And when Onuphrius saw that he was dead, he was sore grieved and downcast, and fell upon the earth and wept bitterly, and buried him afterwards with great reverence, and continued to serve our Lord with prayers, fasting, vigils and many other good practises. And he endured so much, that he often feared he must die; for by day the heat tortured him, and by night the cold, and he suffered much from hunger, until at last, God took pity upon him. Several palms grew near him, and what they bore every year St. Onuphrius gathered together and mixed with herbs and leaves and ate. That was sweet in his mouth like honey. And our Lord comforted him and sent him bread by an angel. And he thanked God with great reverence for that grace.

Good St. Onuphrius, as said, ate at first, only herbs and leaves and lived in caves in the valleys of the mountains, and when he had lived seventeen years in the forest and had suffered much through God, He at last wished to take him away from the world, and give him his reward, and care for him.

At that time there lived a good man by name Paffnucius. He sat alone one day and thought in his heart: 'I will go into the wilderness of the forest and look upon the anchorite monks and learn of their holiness.'

And he went forth and carried bread and water with him, that he might not starve. And he slept upon the road, until the fourth day, when his food was at an end, which he had taken with him.

Then he became very ill, for he had nothing wherewith to nourish himself, and he cried out to God in great bitterness.

Suddenly, a godly grace shone upon him and banished the illness from Paffnucio, which he had. And he was strengthened and arose from the road and walked still another four days, without taking food. Then he was weary again, and fell upon the earth and cried to God.

And immediately he was strengthened by the power of God and he saw a man of wonderful form and beauty, and he was worshipful and tall and of a shining aspect. He stepped toward Paffnucio with a gentle countenance and touched his hands and lips, and restored all his strength to him, and vanished. Then Paffnucio rose suddenly, by the help of God, and walked seventeen days in the desert until God provided a resting place for him. And he was very weary and thought: 'Right miserable am I!'

And as he meditated thus, he saw St. Onuphrius coming in the distance. He was of a horrible aspect, like unto a wild beast; he was rough like a bear, and his hair was so long it covered his whole body and herbs and leaves were about his hips.

When Paffnucio saw St. Onuphrius, he was greatly afraid, and fled to a mountain and hid among the trees. But St. Onuphrius called after him and said: 'Servant of God come hither, and fear not, for I am a human being like thyself!'

And Paffnucio was comforted at those words, and went and fell at his feet.

Then Onuphrius prophesied to him and said: 'Arise, for thou art a child of God; thy name is Paffnucius and thou art a friend of saints.'

And he arose at once and sat down by him, and begged him for love of God to tell him what he was called and from whence he came.

And when Onuphrius had told him all, he continued speaking and said: 'I have lived thus, seventeen years, and during all those years, I have seen no human being but thee, and have received food from no one. If thou wouldst bring God's will to pass, He will provide for thee for He says: 'And seek ye not what ye shall eat, or what ye shall drink. But rather seek ye the Kingdom of God, and all these things shall be added unto you.'

After that, he led Paffnucio three miles further to his cave and let him look at it; palm trees adorned it. Then they said a prayer together and sat there together and talked gently of God, until the sun went down.

Then Paffnucio beheld bread and a little water (appear). Onuphrius knew from that, that the other was ill and weary and spoke: 'Rise up and eat, I see thou art in need of it.'

Paffnucio spoke: 'I will partake only with thee'.

So they ate together, and when they had had enough, there was still a piece remaining. And they passed the whole night in praising God.

Early on the next day, Paffnucius looked and saw that the countenance of Onuphri was changed, and asked him why that was.

And he spoke: 'I must depart from this world, and God has sent thee to bury me, for I shall die soon and my soul will be raised to heaven. Whoever brings an offering to God for my sake, will be freed of all evil spirits and of all human wickedness, and to him will heavenly peace be given, among the angels. And whoever is too poor to make an offering, let him give an alms to the poor, and I will pray that he receive eternal joy. Whoever cannot give an alms, let him give incense, as a sweet fragrance to God, and I will intercede to God for him!'

And Paffnucius spoke: 'Father, I would ask thee, he who can give neither an offering nor alms, nor incense, what shall such an one do to gain thy blessing and thy help?'

And St. Onuphrius answered: 'Let him stand up and raise his hands to God, and say a Pater Noster reverently as I commend, in the name of the Holy

Trinity, and I will intercede for such, that he may
share the heavenly life with all the saints.'

And then Paffnucius begged him, if he should die
to allow him to dwell in his cave.

Then Onuphrius said: 'Not so, for it is God's will
that thou preacheth what thou hast seen and heard
in the wilderness of the forest. And thou willt do
that and be blest.'

Then Paffnucius fell down before him and spoke:
'Father, as God denies thee nothing, because of thy
goodness and great works, I beg thee to implore God
to help me to become like thee, and that in the eternal
life I may be with thee in eternity.'

And St. Onuphrius spoke: 'It shall be as thou
willt.'

And he blessed him.

After that he stood up and prayed, weeping greatly,
and spoke: 'Lord Jesus Christ in thy hands I commend
my spirit!'

And he lay down.

Then a glorious light appeared and enveloped his
holy body, and in the light he departed.

And Paffnucius buried him, and went away from
thence to his own work, and spread the word of
Onuphrius and the salvation of Christ among all people."

The Fools in the Rathhaus.

Such an important part did these fools play at a great banquet which took place about 1480, at the time of strong Duke Christoph, that they were modelled from life in wood and put up on each side of the audience-room, in the Rathhaus.

In old times they loved jokes and quibs, and the fools were allowed to say home-truths, which many a clever and wise man could not do so well today, for they touched upon human weaknesses and false ideals at first jokingly, and then with sarcasm, and they did not spare ambition, and love of power, book-pride, and danger coming from passions of all sorts. In short, they showed mercy to no one, and demonstrated often enough what a short step it is from the serious to the ridiculous, and from the best to the worst, unless one keeps control over oneself.

The fellows must have been very bold, though, for I came across an account of how Duke Albert der Weise, who was at the banquet, was almost angry at first, because one of them asked him in a rhyme about his thread-bare justice to his brother Christoph; but he recovered himself quickly, and smilingly made answer also in rhyme.

The Stone Tablet beside the Giant Door of Unser Frauen Cathedral.

hoever pauses at the giant door between the two steeples of Unser Frauen at Munich, and looks up at the right of the door, will see a stone carving representing our Lord Christ on the Mount of Olives.

That carving is a genuine relic of old Munich and there is a doleful little story connected with it:

In those times, when instead of the present, four-hundred-year-old church, a much smaller one stood in it's place, an honest God-fearing widow lived in Munich. She had a son in whom she placed all her hope, and in whose heart she endeavored to sow the seeds of all virtues. At first he promised well. But as years went on, he fell into bad company, and before his poor mother knew it, he had forgotten all her good old precepts, and when she tried to instill them anew, they were refused, and her son went still further on his reckless path.

At that, she became more severe and kept him shorter in some ways, and he grew just so much more wicked, and once fell into such a rage, that he shouted at her: "Do you think, because you are old and I am young, that I must do as you do? Give me my father's legacy and then we will part!" And because his poor mother did not at once agree, he, in his wantonness, raised his arm, and would have given his own mother a blow. But suddenly his arm became paralized, and for three days, he could not move or bend it.

At that, he was quite subdued and prayed a great deal, and his arm got better, and for a time, he avoided his companions. At last, they came in search of him, and when they were alone, they made fun of him for believing in a sign from God, when he had only demanded his due, for what difference did a little time more or less make.

Those words brought back all his former reckless-ness, and he grew more impudent toward his good mother, and threatened her with all sorts of evil. She reminded him of his duty, and warned him of God's judgment, and, when all that had no result, threw herself, one day, upon her knees before him, imploring him to improve; but he pushed her away and tore open a chest, by main force, taking what it contained of money and valuables, and called out to her: "That is what belongs to me! I am old enough, and tired of your preaching! A merry life brings a happy death!"

At that, the widow lifted her arms to heaven and said: "Lord God, grant that he die like a Christian and not weighed down by Thy curse! The more he lives in revelry, so much the more will I chastise myself and live in self-denial!"

He laughed at that, and exclaimed: "Chastise yourself as much as you like, the more I am spared of it, the better I am pleased!"

Therewith he went his way, leaving his poor mother lying face downward upon the ground, and he continued his wicked life, making great progress in it. But the widow from that time on lived upon almost nothing. Then she went to a good stone-carver, and giving him the sum of money which she had saved, she begged him to carve the Lord Christ on the Mount of Olives in stone. And all the time, the Saviour's prayer that God would let that cup of suffering pass him, kept coming to her mind, for her prayer was the same; namely, that He would spare her draining the cup of suffering to it's dregs, on her son's account.

When a long time had passed and the work was finished, the widow asked permission to have it set into the wall, near the door of the little church; and that was gladly granted her. She prayed before it there, very often and many others did likewise.

While all that was taking place, her godless son had spent all that he had, and had gone from recklessness to crime, falling, at last, into the hands of the police, and was condemned to seven years in a dungeon. During that time, he heard nothing of the outside world, but he reproached himself most bitterly for not having followed his mother's advice, and above all for having sinned against her so miserably; and he swore to God that he would become a different man, and would do the heaviest penance, if He would only grant him the bliss of seeing his mother once more in this life and of begging her forgiveness.

So when he regained his freedom one day, the first thing he did was to hurry home to Thiereck alley, where he supposed his mother was living. But when he reached it, he found other people there, who when they recognized him, exclaimed, "So you are the rascal, who brought so much suffering and disgrace upon the kind widow, that she died of a broken heart! She lies now in the graveyard of St. Mary, under her stone Mount of Olives. Off! and leave this house, for you bring a curse wherever you go!"

Then the widow's son staggered to the little church of St. Mary, and saw the Mount of Olives set into the wall, and saw his mother's grave. He tore his hair and threw himself upon the ground, imploring a sign of forgiveness.

And he went on so for weeks and moons, and grew paler and more wretched all the time, eating and drinking almost nothing at all. So people at last took pity upon him, for anyone could see his bitter remorse. And this one and the other talked with him, and tried to persuade him that his mother in heaven had probably forgiven him.

But he always shook his head, and grew weaker and weaker, so that he could hardly walk, but he did not give up going to his mother's grave.

And once when he passed along, someone said to him: "Today your face is happy, although you are on the same sad errand."

Upon that he answered, "It may well be happy, for in a dream I received the sign for which my soul thirsted. Until now, I have been longing to see my mother and receive a kind look from her, but all this time I have been imploring in vain. Last night, however, she came to me, shining like an angel, with a joyful face, but at the same time, I noticed her eyes were wet. I called out in my dream: "Oh my mother, your eyes are wet from so much suffering and sorrow! Does it not cease then, even in heaven?" Upon that, she looked at me searchingly, and said: "My son, I have often wept as I am weeping now, and much more. But from this moment, it has all passed away, and I have forgotten all the pain." Upon that, I broke out in sobs in my dream, and clung to her and kissed her time and again, and she me, and that waked me. Now I know that she has forgiven me, and I would that I were already with her! So now I am longing for another sign, if God would only send it, that I might know how long I must live!"

Just as he said that, seven strokes of the bell resounded from the little church of St. Mary. They came like a voice from heaven, in answer to his wish. But he did not know whether it meant seven days, weeks, or moons.

It proved to be the first, however, for on the seventh day he died, and was laid beside his mother in the grave.

When the large cathedral of Unser Frauen was built, the stone Mount of Olives was put up again beside the church door.

Requiescant in pace.

Duke Christoph's Stone.

irectly in the passage to the fountain-court of the Residenz, lies that celebrated, old, black stone. Three nails are driven into the wall above it, and an ancient rhyme is carved upon a stone tablet, as follows:

"When after Christ's birth the date was
Fourteen hundred ninety years,
Did Duke Christoph nobly born
A chosen hero of Bavaria
This stone uplift from the flat earth
And fling far off, without exertion.
It weighs three hundred four and sixty pounds,
The stone proves that and the inscription.
Three nails protrude here to the eye,
Let every leaper take a look.
The highest, twelve shoes from the earth,
Duke Christoph of high repute,
Knocked down with his foot.
Kunrath jumped to the other nail,

Ten and half shoes from the earth,
Nine and half, Phillip Springer jumped
To the third nail on the wall.
Who higher leaps will also be renowned —".

If it were merely a question of throwing and jumping, these objects would be rather an ordinary sight. But as it is, they are full of meaning, bearing witness to the kindness and condescension of a princely hero, and moreover to the love in his own heart which he suppressed. That noble hero and duke exerted his great strength and agility for the good of his favorite and faithful servant, Phillip Springer, and thereby gained the hand of Gertraud, the pretty daughter of a wood-sculptor, for him.

Whoever wishes to read all the particulars of the story, how the duke met pretty Gertraud in the Wieskapelle, and how he went to her father on account of the fat counsellor, Florian Hundertpfund, who had fallen in love with the fair maiden, as had been the case with Phillip Springer for a long time, and how a rich stranger, the merchant Kunrath, wanted likewise, to lead Gertraud to the altar, and all that happened up to the time of the trial of who could throw the stone farthest, and jump highest, whoever wishes to read all that will find the tale, precise, clear and merry in the aforesaid "Abenteuer Herzogs Christoph."

There is still another remark to make about the stone.

The above-mentioned throw and jump did not take place on the spot where one sees the stone, nails and tablet now, but in Ludwigs Burg, in the old court-yard, near the long wall at the left, as one enters from Burgstrasse. The stone and tablet remained there until the pretty grotto courtyard was made, and then they were brought over to the old Residenz.

The round, ivy-covered tower which until lately, could be seen just opposite the further side of the Hofgarten, rising up tall and stately from the ditch, bore witness to the rest of the tale, namely the long imprisonment of the knightly duke by his brother Albrecht. Since that part of the Residenz has been built over, on the outside at least, and the ditches filled in, the tower is no longer visible from without. But anyone may go to the furthest corner in the furthest courtyard, and into the tower itself. For the walls of the palace were built around it, leaving the tower intact within, as a memorial; and the ground-level being now so much higher, one walks straight into the selfsame upper room, in which the duke was imprisoned[1]).

It will be told further on what has become of his sword.

The name Christoph, although it had always been a favorite one, was still more loved and used because that noted and adventurous duke had borne it, and the old patron saint of the name, rose ever higher in esteem.

As some of you may not know the church legend of that holy man at all, or at least, not in it's genuine old form, you may be glad to find it here.

"In Canaan, there lived one by the name of Opherus, a heathen like his parents, and exceedingly

[1] In the corner of the Festsaal wing, looking toward Marstallplatz on one side and the Hofgarten on the other.

tall, broad and mighty, and he took no thought of fine clothes, although his father was powerful and rich. Rathermore he went about clad most shabbily, and as much as possible, just as God had made him.

As he continued to grow bigger and stronger all the time, he became so proud of his size and strength, that he wished to serve no other than the most powerful lord, so he made close inquiries as to 'where the mightiest king lived.'

Someone told him of a proud king far away from Canaan. He proved to be so powerful and mighty in land and people that he seemed to Opherus to be the greatest and he offered himself in his service.

One day a strolling player happened by. He sang and acted before the king, and spoke much of the vanities and pleasures of this world, and of other things, which one must guard against. He mentioned the Wicked Enemy often, and whenever the king heard that name, he crossed himself.

When the player had departed, Opherus asked the king what he had meant by the sign he had made on forehead, mouth and breast. Said the king: 'I meant thereby that I protect myself from him whose name was mentioned. You ought to do that in the future also, because he flies away then if he were there invisible. But if one does not make that sign, he gets power over one's soul and brings ruin upon it.'

'If that is so', said Opherus, 'you are afraid of him. His power is greater, then, than yours. Since I know that, I do not wish to be your bondsman any longer, for I serve only the mightiest.'

He forsook the king at that and inquired everywhere for the Wicked Enemy. Everyone knew him by name and was frightened at it, but no one could say where he was.

One day, he happened into a deep forest, and there he saw a group of knights riding toward him, and he who led them wore black armor, and was of a stern and forbidding aspect. But he smiled when he saw Opherus and rode off from the others toward him and said: 'Welcome! You are the mighty Opherus, and I know what you seek and whom! Come and serve me, for I am the most powerful king in the world, the Wicked Enemy!'

Then Opherus said: 'As you know everything about me and are the Wicked Enemy, I will serve you'. And they rode off together, and went into a cave down under the earth. It was dark and barren there, and the new lord of Opherus said to him, he wished to show him his power, and whatever he commanded he would make come to pass.

Said Opherus, 'Then let the ground there become green, and the darkness light!'

Upon that a blithe meadow appeared suddenly, and on it was a lovely garden with trees full of fruit, and strange animals wandered around, and wonderfully plumaged birds flew here and there, and above it all was a light blue like the sky.

Then Opherus said: 'Now I want to see all that destroyed. Let a storm come!'

And it was not long before clouds began to come, and lightning, thunder and hail, and destroyed everything, and darkness was there as at first.

Opherus saw from that and much else, that he had found the most powerful lord and king, and followed him out of the earth, and stayed with him, doing all he was told to do without asking why.

One day, they were going together along a narrow lane near which a cross stood, and when Opherus' master noticed that, he took another road.

Opherus asked him why he went out of the way.

Said the other: 'A cross stands on that road and I do not like to pass it.'

Opherus asked 'Does it mean anything?'

Said the Wicked Enemy: 'To be sure! It reminds me of one, called Jesus Christ, and I cannot bear that!'

'Ho! Ho!' said Opherus, 'If you fly from his sign, He must be more powerful than you! I will not serve you longer, but will serve Him, no matter what He tells me to do!'

Thereupon he left the Wicked Enemy, and inquired everywhere for that mightiest of kings, Jesus Christ.

And some told him He was everywhere, and others said He was in heaven, but all praised His mildness and goodness, although He demanded great sacrifices.

Opherus knew not what to believe and kept on seeking until, one day he came upon a recluse kneeling before a cross, and he thought, 'He can tell me if anyone can", and asked where to find the great king Jesus Christ, whom he wished to serve, and he told of all he had heard.

Said the recluse: 'What you heard is really true. He is in heaven and yet on the earth. He is master of all things, and king of all kings. Whoever wishes to serve him must fast and pray, must kill the sinful life within him, and must be full of meekness toward small as well as great.'

To that Opherus said: 'I do not wish to fast and pray, what good can that do me or Him? I do not know anything about sin, but I will try meekness. So what do you want me to do first?'

Said the recluse: 'Yonder is a wide river, and there is no bridge. If you are in earnest about meekness, take your place there day and night, or build yourself a hut, and when anyone comes, large or small, carry him across without uttering a murmur. Do that for love of your master and king, and if you never see Him in this world you will see Him when you die!'

Said Opherus: 'That is a long way off, and what if I should not see Him even then?'

The recluse answered: 'You must not doubt. Only do your duty, and then I will come and baptise you, and whenever you die after that, your soul will go to heaven, and you will surely see your Lord.'

Upon that, kind Sir Opherus went forth, and toiled day and night carrying people across the river; he hoped the recluse would come and baptise him, and began to fear that he had not done his work aright, and that perhaps he would never see his Lord, either here, or after death, and at last he began to think that the recluse had been making fun of him.

But one night, he heard a voice like that of a child calling out 'Opherus, arise!' Kind Sir Opherus rose from his bed of rushes, at once, but could see no one. The same thing happened a second time, but the third time, he saw a lovely child standing upon the bank, and it said: 'Thou art faithful to thy work, carry me across the river!'

So kind Sir Opherus took the child up on his right arm and his staff in the left, and went into the water. Then the waves began to rise gradually as if they would flood the banks and the child on his arm grew heavier and heavier like lead, and at last the water was so high that Opherus thought he would soon drown, and the child was so heavy, that he could scarcely carry him. Then he stopped a minute and said: 'Child, I do not know whether to turn back or go forward, the water is so deep and the danger so great! And thou art as heavy as if I were carrying the whole world upon me!'

Then the child spoke in it's marvellous voice and said: 'Thou art carrying not only the world, but Him who is Lord of heaven and earth, and King of all Kings! Behold, I myself will baptise thee!' And the child covered Opherus' head with water several times, saying, 'I baptise thee in the name of God the Father and Mine, God the Son and His, and God, the Holy Ghost, Three and yet One. Thou art baptised and thy soul is saved. And thou shalt no longer be called Opherus: I name thee Christopherus, because thou didst carry Me thy Lord Jesus Christ, whom all must serve, not that they be humbled but that they become great and godly.'

And Sir Christopherus said: 'Ah, thy speech is sweet, would that it is no dream!'

And the dear, fair Christchild said: 'No, it is no dream, thou wilt be blessed in my presence. I will give thee a sign. Turn back to the shore and plant thy dry staff in the earth, and as it blossoms, so wilt thou blossom in heaven when thy earthly body has withered away'.

Thereupon the child disappeared from his arm, the water sank to it's former level, and Sir Christopherus returned to the bank, where he stuck his dry staff into the earth, and prayed all night upon his face. And in the morning, when he looked up his staff was full of green leaves and flowers. Upon that, he was filled with joy and exclaimed: 'Oh Lord, because this has come to pass, I believe firmly, and I will teach others, that they likewise believe!' Then he called the recluse to him, and they kneeled down together and prayed with most devout hearts, and the recluse begged Christopherus for his blessing.

He gave it to him accordingly and when he looked again, his staff was bare as before; and he took it and departed from thence and converted many people until his beatified death.''

That is the legend of St. Christopherus and whoever did not know it before, knows it accurately now.

The Tabernacle of the Holy Wafer in the Large Cemetery.

W ithin the graveyard near Sendling Gate is a tabernacle with a curious history. It stands on the right of the path infront of the church. Formerly, it was in quite another place, namely in the city, near Salvator, or, as it is now called, the Greek church, and before that it was in still another place.

Here is a short account of it and of what is associated with it.

The column with it's little tower is connected with the robbery of a holy wafer from the church of St. Mary which an old woman, at the beginning of Ao. Dom. 1400, committed, in order, it was said, to give it over to a Jew, who was waiting for her outside the city.

Stung by her conscience she dropped the sacred object outside Schwabing Gate, which stood at the beginning of what is now Briennerstrasse, where some people found it, and carried it back in a solemn procession to the little church of St. Mary.

A small chapel, in honor of our Saviour, was built on the spot where it was found, and the gate after that, often went by the name of Unser Herrn Gate, and the small chapel was called the Saviour or Salvator chapel.

Later in Ao. Dom. 1493, when Duke Albrecht der Weise was ruling, certain necessary changes were made in the city, and they took away the small chapel and put up the above-mentioned column in it's place. Some are of the opinion it had been there for a long time already, but that is not true. The Duke commanded a stone-sculptor to carve four scenes around the top; the woman who stole the wafer; the crowning of Christ with thorns; the bearing of the cross; and the crucifixion. It has suffered much from the weather but a good deal is still distinct.

The inscription runs thus: Albrecht, Markgrave of the Rhein, Duke of Upper and Lower Bavaria caused this work to be made. In the year of 1494.

But it did not occur to the Duke to deprive Munich of a house of God, and he decided to build a large church in place of the small one, on the so-called Frauen graveyard. So they tore down the small chapel and built the church with the tall pointed steeple which stands there today. And in memory of the chapel which had been there before, they called it Salvator church.

After that, the aforesaid column must have been moved to Frauen graveyard, on account of changes which were taking place outside the gate.

Years later, Duke Wilhelm IV. caused a stone monument to be erected near it, with a lantern in which an eternal light burned behind red glass.

Then the two monuments stood side by side many years, until in the course of time, the Frauen grave-yard was abolished, and everything in it carried away; the two monuments found humble resting-places in the large cemetery outside Sendling Gate, where they were placed not far apart[1]).

Up to the end of the eighteenth century, there were two little painted tablets at the entrance to Frauen graveyard, whereon the arrest of the old wo-man and the raising of the Host were pictured. Later they came into the possession of an old member of the clergy, at whose house I saw them, when I was a small boy. I do not know where they are now, would that I did!

While we are speaking of the old Frauen grave-yard, and the two monuments, something else may as well be mentioned.

Namely, near the two monuments stood the old chapel of St. George, which Duke Albrecht built at the same time with Salvator church. In that chapel, nobles of high birth, were dubbed knights of St. George. The knighting occurred then, as at present, on the day of St. George; but it takes place now in the court chapel of the old Residenz.

---

1) They are now in the garden of the National Museum, Hof II.

On such occasions, members of the high nobility walk through the halls of the Residenz and court-yards to the chapel, and every detail is according to old tradition.

The princes walk with them and the king, who is master of the order, likewise. The dubbing takes place with the sword of Duke Christoph, for we in Munich possess that as well as his shield, which were brought back here when he died on the journey home from his pilgrimage.

One sees at a glance, from all these things, that St. George has never been counted among Bavaria's less important saints. Still if it should come to the point, it would not surprise me if some one of you did not know anything positive about him. Consequently his genuine old legend may not be out of place here, for it is amusing as well as edifying.

It is written down thus; St. George was a knight, and son of a count of Palestine, and holds a banner in his hand, about which is the following history.

"In times of old when Pope Marcellus ruled, Sir St. George fought against all sorts of heathen and won victory after victory.

It was on the eve of another battle at Cappodoci, and St. George had such a small number of men that the heathen mocked at his handful of soldiers.

Thereupon he commanded his men to kneel down and pray. The heathen misunderstood that, and sent over a messenger who said, 'You are desperate with fright, we can see as much as that; surrender and make an offering to our gods, and it may go well with you; if not, you are all doomed to die.'

Said St. George: 'Not at all! You, not we, are doomed to die, and we are in nowise desperate, we are only praying for a sign from heaven.' Said the same heathen: 'And what is that supposed to be?'

Answered St. George: 'You impudent heathen, I will tell you! We are waiting for a sign which will make ten men out of one of us, and I see the sign coming already!'

Said the heathen: 'I see nothing, and you see nothing either, you impudent Christian. But even if we both saw anything, and your magician god should make a hundred out of one of you, we would beat you, even then, for we are too many for you!'

Thereupon he went back to the heathen camp.

But St. George looked up joyfully to heaven, for it had opened and an angel was floating down holding in his hand a banner upon which was a red cross. He gave the banner to St. George saying, 'In hoc signo vinces! Each one of your men shall become a hundred and each thousand of the heathen, one. Thou surely dost understand what that means'.

Upon that, Sir St. George and his men set out and marched toward the heathen camp, shouting, 'Jesus Christ of Nazareth, who fights against Thee!'

The heathen were furious at that, and began the battle expecting to mow the Christians down like grass. But dear St. George held his banner high in the air and slashed at the heathen with his sword, his men doing the same, so that the battle was horrible, and one could see the dust from it, three miles away.

Innumerable heathen were slain, and their souls went downwards; many of St. George's men were also slain but their souls went up to heaven; at last, the heathen were entirely wiped out, except one man, their commander. He escaped and spread the news about the banner from heaven, and the victory of the Christians, from one end of heathendom to the other.

Many of them took it deeply to heart, and destroyed their idols, and became good Christians, and together with their commander, they went over to the ranks of St. George and fought with him for the honor and glory of our Lord Christ. And thus did the word of the angel come to pass."

Another legend of St. George is: "The Roman emperor, Diocletian, had him arrested once, and left, bound and fastened, in the hut of a poor old woman. It was winter outside, and there was much snow and it was bitter cold.

When St. George and the woman were alone, the latter said, 'I am sorry for you, and if I had anything I would give it you, but hunger and sorrow are all I possess, and my child is ill and blind. If only he could be cured, but there seems to be no help. However, I will go and pray to the gods, at least, perhaps someone will give me some bread then, otherwise I and my child must perish, and I can give you nothing'.

Said St. George: 'Your gods cannot help you, but mine can'.

And she replied: 'In what can your god help? He is no god, for otherwise you would not be in chains here'.

When St. George was alone, he prayed. Then an angel came and loosed his chains and said: 'Raise thine arms gently up against the door-posts, and the old woman will be greatly benefited thereby.'

So dear St. George touched the door-posts with his arms and they turned into a tree standing alone, with wide-spreading branches, the roof became a network of foliage, wonderful fruit hanging from each twig and everywhere beautiful birds were singing. The ground was a cheery greensward and a table of ruby stood upon it: on the table was bread of heaven and a golden cup of wine.

When the poor woman came home through the snow, and looked in, she was greatly amazed, but St. George told her to eat and drink. She did so, and heavenly fruit fell upon the table, according to the sort she wished for, and she drank of the wine, but her tears fell into the cup and she said: 'In my hunger, I forgot my child, I must bring him and feed him also. Ah! If he could only see all this magnificence and glory; but your god cannot do that, if he could, mine would be nothing compared to him!'

Said St. George: 'Cease lamenting, for it has happened!'

And when the woman hurried to her child's bed, it was healthy instead of ill and looked up smilingly to her, as if it could see it's mother. The poor woman could hardly believe her senses and carried it out of the closet, to where the beautiful tree was, and when the child saw the twigs and fruit, it stretched out its little hands toward them. At that, belief in her child's recovery, and in the god of St. George, filled the woman's heart and she exclaimed, 'My gods are helpless and cruel but yours is good and almighty!'

5*

And she fed her child, blissfully, with heavenly bread and wine, and then hurried away with it, through the snow, to make known to the people what had happened.

And many people came, and they all found room in the hut which had become a bower, and like the poor mother, they wished to be baptised.

St. George would have done it with great joy, and suddenly dew began to fall upon the green grass and St. George caught it in the hollow of his hand and baptised each and all. And they departed in bliss for their souls were changed, and their hearts full of God's joy.

When the emperor heard of what had happened, and was told about the tree with birds and fruit, and about the wine and bread and all the rest, he wished to see it for himself and went there through the snow. And when he entered, all the birds became silent, and the leaves and grass withered away and the tree and everything else vanished, the hut standing there again, as it was before. He was horrified at that, and fled out into the snow and winter. But St. George gave the poor woman and her child his blessing, and went his way, for his time of suffering was not yet come."

Another about St. George is:

"Once the heathen said, 'Pray to our sun- god, if not, you must die.'

Said St. George: 'If he come to me.'

Said the heathen: 'Listen to him, he thinks our god will go to him!'

Said St. George: 'I will show you then'. And he

said to a Christian child, 'Go over and tell him to get down from his stone and follow you, and if he does not obey, take this rod and force him!'

Then the stone god walked along and the child drove him with the rod. The heathen were amazed, and full of anger and fury, but dear St. George took no notice of that, and said to the stone god: 'I ask thee in the name of God, art thou the sun- god, or who art thou?'

The other began to tremble mightily and said, 'Must I say it? I am one of those whom God drove out of heaven! Wait, I will revenge myself on thee!'

Said St. George: 'I hold thee in little fear, but I will that thou showest thyself in thy real shape'.

Upon that, the Evil One stood there in his horrid form, before the eyes of all, and cried out for pity.

But good St. George called out, 'Descend to the deepest hell!'

At that, the earth opened and a flame darted out of it, and the Evil One sank out of sight with a loud shriek, and the heathen raised a hue and cry and fled from St. George."

And again.

"Once the emperor wished to cast a slur at St. George's power; so he caused a coffin to be brought, containing the bones of many heathen, and said; 'As you are so powerful, bring them to life!'

Said St. Georg: 'Not I but another, who is higher than I'.

And after he had prayed, all the bones went together as they belonged, and grew into bodies and a number of human beings became visible, and they said they had been lying there 313 years, waiting for him who should save their souls.

Said the emperor: 'I am he, then, for I have waked you through the power of my magician Georgius, yonder.'

Answered one: 'You are a liar, for the angels of God do not praise a magician and we heard them praising St. George. He shall baptise us now, and our souls will be saved'.

Then St. George made the sign of the cross over the earth and a spring came forth out of it, and then he baptised those who were risen from the dead; and they were full of gratitude. And he said: 'Now you are Christians, and I ask you, do you desire to live a second time upon the earth and die for your faith?' And they answered with one voice: 'We wish it.'

Said St. George, 'Your good-will shall stand for works, and for that reason you shall not die in suffering, but in peace', and he made the sign of the cross over them and said: 'Lie down again in your coffin, and your souls shall go up to heaven and paradise. Give greeting to my father, mother, and my brother for me, and the Virgin Mary and above all my Lord Jesus Christ. I thank him in all humility for my courage!'

Then the others said, 'Gloria in excelsis.' And suddenly, they were there no longer, but had become a heap of bones again, in the coffin. Thereupon, the emperor was afraid to stay there longer and went away".

Afterwards St. George had to fight with a dragon; and that was as follows.

"At that time, there was a horrible dragon in the land of Silena. It was near a lake, and poisoned all the water, and it devoured any beast or human being who came near; and if nothing came for some time, it crept into the city. The people in the city did not like that at all, and preferred to go out and feed it with two lambs. But the more lambs it devoured, the more it wanted, until there was hardly a lamb left in the city. At that they decided to cast lots and whoever drew it should be offered up to the dragon, with a lamb.

And one day there was no lamb to be found and the lot fell upon the king's daughter.. The king wept and begged for eight days space of time. And when that had passed, he begged for more, but it was of no use, he had to take leave of his daughter; and they parted from each other in great distress, and the virgin went to the lake and wept bitterly, waiting for death as soon as the dragon came that way.

Meanwhile dear Sir St. George came riding by, and when he saw the sorrowful virgin, he dismounted from his steed, and asked her what her grief was.

She told him and then begged him to escape, for there was no help for her. He comforted her in the name of God, and meanwhile the dragon crept out of the lake. The virgin was sore afraid, but St. George swung himself upon his steed, made the sign of the cross, and riding at the dragon, slashed at it with his sword, so that it grew weak, and fell over in it's black blood.

Then dear Sir George said: 'It is not quite dead, take your girdle, bind it around it's neck and lead it into the city.' The virgin did accordingly and St. George rode at her side. When the people saw the dragon tied to the girdle, they raised a great cry and wanted to flee. But St. George called them back and said, 'I have come to you that you may be saved from the danger to your souls, as you are saved from the danger to your bodies. For that reason I destroy this monster.'

And he drew his sword a second time, and pierced the dragon to death, and commanded it to be buried in the earth outside the city.

At that, all the people of Silena were converted and the king built a church, and when they broke the earth for it, a miraculous spring burst forth, and when St. George had taught them all Christianity, he baptised them, and rode away from them."

And now comes the last about St. George, which happened after he had died for our Lord Christ.

"The heathen laid siege to the city of Jerusalem, and the Christians could scarcely save themselves. Then they carried the bones of St. George up onto the city-wall and the Christians summoned courage at the sight of that; but the heathen fell into a greater fury, and shot and stormed all the worse, and they were nearly a hundred thousand.

Thereupon St. George, the knight of God, appeared in the air, wearing a snow-white robe over his armor, and carrying his white banner with the red cross, and he called out in a joyful voice to the Christians: 'Courage, good sirs, we shall conquer with the help of God!' And he descended upon the city-wall and waved his sacred sign on high in the air.

And when the Christians saw that, they were all filled with joy and fell upon the heathen with might and main, and a regular massacre ensued, and as many of the heathen as were able, fled, for half of them were slain."

Those are the chronicles of St. George and his victories.

Duke Sigmund's Memorial Stone.

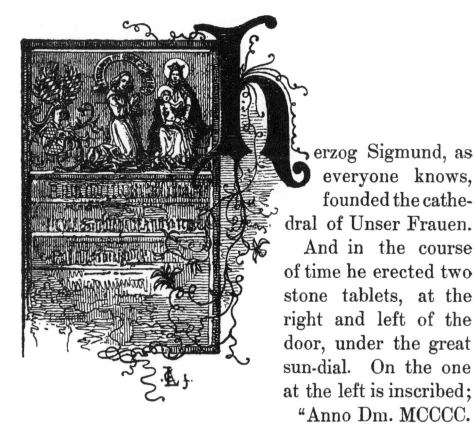

Herzog Sigmund, as everyone knows, founded the cathedral of Unser Frauen. And in the course of time he erected two stone tablets, at the right and left of the door, under the great sun-dial. On the one at the left is inscribed; "Anno Dm. MCCCC. In that year this building was begun, eight days after Candlemass of Our Lady."

Anno 1488 the building was completed.

The epitaph on the architect's gravestone in the south end under one of the steeples is this:

"Ao. Dom. 1488, on Monday after St. Michael's day, master Jörg (Gankoffen) of Halsbach, architect of this house of worship to Our Lady, died, who with the help of God and his own hand, laid the first, the middle and the last stone of this building, he lies buried here with his wedded spouse. God be gracious to them."

At the right of the aforesaid church door, exactly opposite the tablet commemorating the building of the church, Duke Sigmund raised a tablet for himself. One sees him in kneeling posture on it, and the Latin inscription underneath speaks of his reverence for God and devotion to the Virgin Mary, for whom he had vowed to endow and build the church.

The two Latin lines at the top,

"Clam fortuna ruit fragile pede, tempus et hora,
Nostraque sunt semper facta dolenda nimis",

proclaim the briefness of happiness and the imperfection and vanity of all earthly deeds.

When the above-mentioned Duke chose that inscription, he was 29 years old, and a few years before, he was supposed to have been deeply in love with a maiden of the middle-class, and he declared himself ready for any sacrifice if he could win her for his wife. Then, as is well known he abdicated in favor of his brother, Albrecht der Weise. From hints here and there, it seems the fair maiden had already been led to the altar by someone else; at any rate everyone knows that the Duke remained unmarried his whole life, and so it is possible that those two lines have a particular meaning. Namely, that the Duke intended to immortalize thereby the sorrow of his disappointed love, and the uselessness of his abdication.

But at any rate Duke Sigmund seems to have taken courage later, for accounts tell of how he spent his time at castle Blutenburg, not far from Munich, where he led a merry life and cared much for fair women, good *cantores*, and such things.

There is no space for more particulars on that subject here.

The Tombstone of the Master of Nürnberg.

nder the big sun-dial of Unser Frauen, on the wall at the left of the door, is a venerable old tombstone. It belongs to the blind musician Conrad Paumann, knight, and native of Nürnberg, a man who was equally remarkable for his talent, character and misfortune.

The rude art of olden times has carved him there in red marble, sitting at the organ, wearing a long coat, and close-fitting cap, his fingers touching the keys. Various sorts of instruments are to be seen, and by the turn of his head, the sculptor probably meant to indicate that the master was listening intently to the tones. When one considers what it means to be blind and yet to advance so high in the art of music, that emperors and princes send for one, and make one gifts of rich silk and velvet robes bordered with fur, and a costly sword and other honors, to say nothing of their sincere praise, when one thinks of all that, it should surely be a spur to industry and perseverance.

But that was not all, for Master Conrad dictated a remarkably beautiful hymn which is now in the Royal Library, which would give many a one great enjoyment if it could be heard now.

His life at Nürnberg was full of strange, admonitory incidents, and it was not less so, after God's dispensation had brought him to Munich. Here, it was ordained that he should bring about a reconciliation between Duke Albrecht the Third, that same Albrecht, whose sweetheart, Agnes Bernauer, was drowned at his father's command, and his duchess, Anna von Braunschweig. That happened through a couple of terse verses which the Duke wrote and which the blind master set to music, and caused to be sung, just when the obstinate Anna was saying her prayers for the night. She supposed she was alone when suddenly the melody and the well-known words fell upon her ear, and through the door, she saw the singers and pages holding candles, and Master Conrad, and her husband, with whom she had long wished to make up the quarrel, had she not been too proud.

That pride caused her bitter remorse many times later; let us take warning by it and be the first to make peace after a quarrel, for life is so short, and the more hearts we win, the richer we are.

The aforesaid Master of Nürnberg had a rival,

an Italian musician by name Fra Solina, whom he conquered in an organ competition, and, when the Italian accused him of witchcraft, in a duel by swords, as well.

The master had a step-daughter who had been in love for many years with Master Lindenast of Nürnberg, but she intended keeping it a secret until the death of Conrad because she could not bear to leave him. The master discovered it, however, and gave her his heartfelt blessing in recognition of her noble conduct. And so the two lovers were happily united after their long probation. The wicked Italian, however, who had had his sinful eye upon Cornelia for a long time and who tried to murder Conrad in the old castle courtyard, died in prison.

The corner house opposite the bank, in Theatinerstrasse belonged to Conrad.

His epitaph runs thus; "Anno Dom. MCCCCLXXIII on the evening of St. Paul's conversion, there died and lies buried here, the greatest artist of all instruments and music, Master Conrad Pauman, knight, a native of Nürnberg, and blind from birth. God be merciful to him!"

St. Michael, Short of Money.

oubtless the short steeple, at the back of St. Michael's church, is what is meant by that saying. This same church of St. Michael was built by Duke Wilhelm V, the cornerstone being laid on April 18, 1583. The name of the architect was Andreas Gundlfinger, but a Jesuit priest, Valerian, from Italy, and one from Munich, by name Simon Hiendl, also had a good deal to do with it, while he who really had the responsibility of the whole thing was a certain Müller, whose effigy is now in the sacristy.

There is a saying about this Müller, that he built the marvellous dome at his own risk, and it was considered an unequalled master-work. But when the Duke commanded that a couple of cannon be fired off in the church, as a test of it's stability, the aforesaid Müller, sure as he was of his work, was seized

with fright and fled, never to be seen again. There
may be some truth in the story, but one thing is sure,
that he came back again, for legal documents exist,
which give an account of how Müller defended himself against certain charges, a little later, in regard
to the steeple.

But about the steeple itself; at first St. Michael's
church was not so long as it is now, and a steeple
stood at the back; the statue of St. Michael was on
it, which is now between the two doors on the front.
That was Anno Dom. 1590, shortly before the church
was to be consecrated. But the steeple fell, and un-
friendly Jesuits called it the "punishment of God and
anger of St. Michael", because Jesuits had not been
consulted in the matter enough. But Duke Wilhelm
answered, "That is not true! More probably the
church is not large enough for Him." And he commanded the church to be made longer and another
steeple built at the back. Any one can see how far
they got with it. For after the Duke had spent a
great deal upon the church, he suddenly stopped, and
so the epithet "short of money" has always been
attached to the steeple, although many people aver
it was not built higher for fear of lightning.

An anecdote about the first, tall tower is as follows:

When the Duke was choosing the architects, a
court-architect, Wendel Dietrich, was deeply offended
at being left out, because he had hoped for the place
too. But he said nothing disagreeable and only kept
a close watch over the plans and sketches, and particularly those of the steeple. When he saw how thick
it was to be and it's base, he could not contain his

long-repressed, well-meaning indignation any longer, and in answer to a question of the Duke, he burst out with, "I will only say this much, if they do not change the base, and make the whole steeple thicker, it will fall down upon their precious heads!" Naturally, that speech soon spread about. The Duke asked the architects about the matter, and they ran down Wendel Dietrich to such a degree, and made it so hot for Wilhelmus that the latter sent word to Wendel, "He must keep quiet for the future and reserve his faultfinding to himself, and the ducal displeasure, moreover, rested upon him." They did not let Wendel forget that severe reproof and went on building. Wendel, after that, kept quiet, but when this one or the other asked him jokingly, "Well, Master Wendel, will the steeple fall soon?" he answered, "Keep quiet, or the ducal displeasure will rest upon you".

When the steeple was at last finished, and a crowd of people often stood around looking at it, Wendel Dietrich was frequently among them, and a friendly joke, poked at him now and then, did not seem to annoy him.

But once he was standing there with his hands behind his back, when the Duke and all the architects came that way unnoticed by Wendel, until the Duke tapped him lightly on the shoulder and said, "Ay Wendel! What about my steeple? There it is, and it does not look like falling!"

Said Wendel, lifting his hat: "Not today. First, that small crack up there must become a large one. God save you, Herr Herzog!" So saying, he glanced up at the steeple again and went his way.

Said Gundlfinger: "Your Highness, the man gets more impudent every day! What is that nonsense about cracks?"

When the Duke and the architects, the clergy and other people looked carefully, they discovered a tiny crack, and the Duke said, "That cannot be good, Gundlfinger, what if Wendel should be right after all!"

To make a long story short, before the day was over, the little crack had grown wider, and on the next evening every one was saying, "If that continues, the steeple will certainly fall!" Other bad signs appeared and the entire city was in the greatest excitement; all possible precaution was taken so that too much damage should not happen, and then suddenly the whole steeple collapsed, with a crash and rumble, that one could hear in Dachau, if not further; at the cost of much trouble, they had lowered the St. Michael from the roof of the steeple and so, saved it.

Upon that, Gundlfinger, and the priests, Hiendl and the Italian Valerius, were in no very happy mood, and Duke Wilhelm called them to him together with Wendel. Then he gave them all, clergy and laity, a good piece of his mind, "with visible discontent and deep and most apparent annoyance, in no very gracious words". Then he turned to Wendel and said, "If you were so sure and certain from the beginning that the steeple would fall, why did you not make more noise about it? I have a good mind to withdraw my favor from you!"

Said Wendel Dietrich: "Ah, Your Highness, one never knows which way to turn for favor. In the first place I lost it because I said too much, and now

6*

I lose it, because I did not say enough! It is hard to do right in this blasphemous world. With all due respect, with or without favor, if you had taken me, all this would not have happened."

Said Gundlfinger: "He is going a little too far in his impudence! Have him imprisoned, Your Highness!"

Said the Duke: "By no manner of means! If I send any one to prison, it will not be Wendel Dietrich, but all of you, for you do not know how to build, you have proved that. Therefore you may begin to build all over again, and under his command, for I restore my favor to him, and to you the Dev—, God forgive me, a farthing, for your work!"

And now, as St. Michaels is such a wonderfully fine house of God, it may interest some of you to hear about it's consecration.

It took place on the 6th of July, 1597, and in the presence of a great number of princes and noblemen. Their names were as follows:

The holy Bishop of Freising, Bartolomäus,
The church founder, Duke Wilhelm the Fifth,
His wife, Duchess Renata of Lorraine,
The Prince-Elector, Maximilian,
His wife, Elizabeth of Lorraine,
The church founder's brother,
Duke Ferdinand,
The Cardinal and Bishop of Regensburg, Philip-
 pus, and
The assistant of the Archbishop and Elector of
 Cologne, Ferdinand, both sons of the founder,
Another son of the same, Albertus,

His daughters, Maria Anna, and Eleonora Magdalena,

His sisters, Maria Maximiliana and Maria, widow
of Archduke Carl of Austria,

And many younger people, such as Archduke
Ferdinand, who was Roman Emperor later,

The Grand-master of the German Order, Leopold,

The Bishop of Passau and Brixen, Carolus,

Five young Archduchesses, Maximiliana, Eleonora,
Margaretha, Constantia and Magdalena,

Further, the Landgrave of Leuchtenberg, Georg
Ludwig, and many other illustrious lords and
ladies.

The sermon was delivered by Cardinal Duke
Philipp, and after the dedication ceremony, there was
a splendid feast spread for 1700 persons, in all the
halls, passages and garden of the Jesuit monastery.
The next Friday, the scholars in the Jesuit school
near the church, of whom there were nine hundred,
gave a very instructive comedy, namely the "Struggle
between the Archangel Michael, and the Devil's Grand-
duke Lucifer". The music was by the new choir-
director of St. Michael's, Georg Victorini, who had
the reputation of being a very clever composer, and
who sustained that reputation, especially in the Devil's
Fall. "And on the whole", someone recorded, "the
senses and eyes of the spectator were so bewitched
by the rarest inventions, and most lifelike imitations,
beautifully painted scenes, and artfullymade machines,
rich clothing and the great number and skilfulness of
the actors, that the eight hours time which it lasted,
seemed only too short."

So much for the consecration of St. Michael's church.

As for the crypt of St. Michael's, a goodly number of princes are buried there. Some of the oldest, are the founder, Wilhelm V, and his wife, Renata of Lorraine, and his son the great Elector Maximilian, with his two wives, Elizabeth of Lorraine and Anna of Austria.

But to continue; there is a saying about the Jesuit monastery[1]) near by, to this effect: "Somewhere near a flight of stairs, a treasure is concealed, which the Jesuits buried a short time before they were compelled to leave the monastery. A mason, just before he was about to die, told about it in a very clear and lucid manner. One night some one came for him, and after bandaging his eyes, led him here and there in a round-about way to a certain place, where he was told to wall up several chests and boxes, and from all that happened, he judged it was near some stairs. As he was being led out, several things made him think he was in the Jesuit monastery, one being that his right foot stumbled against a loose floor-tile. The next day, he went through the passages of the monastery and found the loose Kelheimer tile, just where he expected. That and some other incidents left no doubt in his mind, but he was silent about it, because in the first place, he felt kindly toward the fathers, and in the second, they had extracted a vow of silence from him."

---

1) The building at the left of the church, which is now the Academy of Sciences.

The story has a good deal of truth in it most probably, because one does not usually tell lies just before one's death, and so, no doubt the treasure is still lying there, in the monastery. The question is, near which stairs. It is only to be hoped the right one will find it, for one could conquer many difficulties with that treasure.

The Old Residenz.

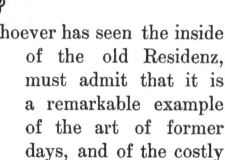

hoever has seen the inside of the old Residenz, must admit that it is a remarkable example of the art of former days, and of the costly splendor, existing at the time of Elector Max I, as well as of his grandson, Max Emanuel, and his great-grandson, Karl Albert or Emperor Karl the Seventh.

So much exists in documents and pictures about this old Residenz and it's riches and buildings, which were formerly connected with the Fürstenberg, and it's grounds, that it would not be difficult for me to give a long account, and even at this day, to cause some astonishment.

But some one did it so much better, as far back as Anno 1698, namely, "Sir Anthoni Wilhelm Ertel von Lebenburg, knight of the Order of St. Lazari in Jerusalem and Bethany, Mediator for the holy Roman Empire, and general syndic", in the "Kurbayrischen

Atlantis", a book, which many are acquainted with and read.

So I shall take good care not to attempt warmer and more high-flown words than those of that amiable and loyal man, when he speaks of the Residenz and of the reigning lord, Max Emanuel, who as I have said, did much to make the Residenz still more beautiful.

And it is only proper that he speak here in my place, as an illustration of how much more advanced they were at that time, in the art of bestowing praise, than we, who in our pride of style, do not know where to find words enough.

In speaking of the riches of the Chamber of Treasures, for instance, who is there today, who could outstrip his description of the pearls alone, in aptness and terseness:

"I could tell of 500 treasures of monstrous rarity, whereby your eyes would swim with the wonder of it, but some secret cause has stopped the flow of my pen. So it must suffice me to say that all five human senses of the mortal, who has the good fortune to behold those treasures, are fully occupied."

And the same may be said of the passage where the good knight of St. Lazarus speaks of the tilting-yard, or old riding-school, which stood where the shops are now.

"That is a glorious building where all the chivalry of Bavaria gives many a proof of valiant courage. And in that place, our victory-crowned Emanuel has often practised his hand with the pointed lance and gleaming sword, that hand which later, in his heroic bravery, he often colored in the unclean blood of

Turkish dogs and moon-struck beasts at Vienna, Gran, Neuhäusel, Waizen and other places, and thereby crowned his Bavarian lions with many splendid laurel-wreaths."

That finished eulogist is still more eloquent about the Elector in another part.

"Our descendants will read with astonishment in more than a thousand accounts of how Maximilian, the mighty hero, reaped glorious laurels for himself, three years at a time, during the siege of Vienna by the bloodthirsty Turks, where his courage and watchful endurance became world renowned, and his remarkable genius can never be enough praised. And since Emanuel is above all Nobiscum Deus, I can comfort my beloved country with the promise that through Emanuel and by means of him, we shall always have the support of heaven, and always be sure of victory. And since Maximilian Emanuel, changing the letters, reads, Maximum Lenamen in alis, so may we take still more comfort in the thought that Bavaria rests safe and blissful under the wings of that great electoral phoenix, risen from the ashes of the first Maximilian in Bavaria, and the smoke of the rare virtues which adorned his noble father Ferdinand Maria — — and his wife (first) Maria Antonia Josepha Benedicta Rosalia Petronella — a true mirror of all virtues, nourished by the milk of Austrian meekness, and the blood of Spanish glory, an image of all gracious traits, and a genuine pomegranate of many hundreds of most excellent beauties of the soul."

The Red Light.

t has already been proved that the little tower with the fist, near Sendling Gate is of particular interest to Munich people. And formerly there was still another story associated with it. The headsman of Munich played a part in the tale, which was as follows:

It is to be hoped that no innocent person was ever purposely expedited from this world to the other, here at Munich. Still it came to pass, at one time or another during the course of centuries, that a person who had done no harm, came before the court-of-justice, and the judges made a mistake; stranger things have happened.

At any rate, when an innocent person was killed, it never remained a secret.

For, in the middle of the next night, the little Faust Tower gleamed in a blood-red light, and at the

same time, three heavy thuds like those of the headsman's sword, resounded upon the executioner's house,
which was formerly in the square near the little tower.

When the headsman heard the three thuds, and
saw the blood-red light, he never failed to open the
door and ask who had knocked and where the red
light came from, for that had been the custom since
his great-grandfather's and still earlier times. The
next thing he did, was to kneel down and say one
Pater Noster and Ave Maria after another, in a loud
voice, until one o'clock sounded from the city, and
on the stroke, the red light faded and disappeared.
Then he returned to his pillow, but it is easy to
fancy that he did not sleep, and the next morning,
he notified the counsel of what had happened.

Upon that, all the people betook themselves to
churches and chapels, for they knew the three thuds
and red light meant that an innocent person had been
punished, and there they prayed earnestly for his
soul, and still more so that the guilty one should be
discovered.

That happened several times. The first time it
was a goldsmith, who lived near the Beautiful Tower,
which no longer exists. The second, a maidservant,
who slept in a little room at the top of a house in
Dienerstrasse. Both of them were killed though innocent, because it looked as if they had taken valuables which did not belong to them, while the real
thieves were a jackdaw and a magpie.

On the ridge-pole of one of the houses, there is
a magpie to be seen at the present day, though many
mistake it for a crow. There is no account of what

happened to the jackdaw and magpie, although there are records of two other cases, in which the real criminels suffered punishment of death.

The first case happened as follows, and about two hundred years ago.

Two cousins quarrelled about an inheritance in Munich. There was much talk about the affair, and at last one of them won the case, and the other received nothing. When the one came suddenly into so much money, he began to drink and gamble in the Bürger winehouse, and Ammerthal inn, and other public houses, and never left the table until the house was closed for the night. Then he staggered along Neuhauserstrasse homewards, sometimes his friends having to hold him up, and when he reached Eisenmannstrasse, where his cousin lived, he began to jeer and mock, his companions doing the same.

One night he had been throwing dice with two strange merchants in Ammerthal inn, and had won a good deal of money.

Afterward he went out alone, and people heard him jeering and making a noise at his cousin's door. But that was nothing unusual. Suddenly, though, they heard something else, he seemed to be calling for help.

People appeared at windows here and there and a few opened their doors and hurried out, and when they reached the spot, they found the rich cousin lying in his blood. But the poor cousin was there too, and the other was still wrestling with him, as weak as he was, and saying between his groans, "So that is the way you revenge yourself, by robbing me of the gold gulden! It will cost you your life and vultures will devour you!"

The poor cousin swore to him and those standing around that he had come out just as they had done, when he heard the cries for help; he had found his cousin there in the darkness, just as he was now; at first he had tried to catch the murderer, but he had already escaped, so he came back to help his cousin.

Neither his cousin, who died very soon, nor anyone else believed a word of what he said, and he was arrested and thrown into Falken Tower; and when the case had begun, the fact that the money was nowhere to be found did not help him in the least. For as he himself had said, that at first he had hurried away from the scene of the murder to catch the murderer, they regarded that as an excuse, and thought he had taken that way to hide his booty. In short, he was found guilty of the dreadful deed, and brought to the block, where he pleaded innocent until the last minute, but no one believed him.

At midnight, however, when Master Martin, the headsman, was sleeping the sleep of the just, there came a sudden thud upon his door so that he jumped up and listened; after awhile, a second one came, and then a third, and when he looked out, he saw the square, the city-wall, and the little tower glowing in a blood-red light.

Upon that, he fell upon his knees and prayed according to the custom in such times, steadily until one o'clock, when the light faded. Then he sought his pillow again, resolving to go the first thing in the morning, to notify the burgomaster and chief justice of what had happened; but sleep did not come to him, as had been the case once with his great great-grandfather.

Suddenly, he heard steps in the square outside, and they stopped before his door, and then there was a rapping upon the door and window-shutters, and the call, "Open Master Martin, open!"

When he heard that, he thought, "The dangerous time is over, for that is no ghost or spirit from the other world, but someone from this; who knows what may be happening in the city". So he rose quickly and throwing on his clothes, he unbolted the door and asked, "Who is there, and what is the trouble?"

Then he saw a man with dishevelled hair and a feverish look who said: "What are you staring at, dont you know me?"

Said the headsman: "I recognize you now. You are Dolwein! But what makes you look so wild?"

Said the other: "Did you see the red light and hear the three thuds?"

Said Master Martin "My soul! I heard and saw it all, and he whom I beheaded was innocent. Did you hear it all too? But courage! for God will surely show us the right one!"

Replied the other: "That has already happened, for I am the right one, the murdered man's friend. I killed him and escaped from the poor cousin, who pursued me. Then he went back and was arrested instead of me, and then killed instead of me".

The headsman asked, "Where is the money?"

And the other, "There it is, take it, and arrest me, and take me either to the Rathhaus or prison this very night; I shall find no peace until I get the punishment I deserve".

So the headsman could no longer doubt his word, and told him to march along an arm's length in front of him, for the law forbade him to touch him until his sentence had been pronounced. The other agreed to it and marched in front to the sentry at Sendling Gate, whom the headsman called out and delivered the fellow over to.

Then he was put in chains and led into the city to Falken Tower; he stayed there until morning; then he was brought before the court, where he confessed the whole affair clearly, and in a short time justice was visited upon him, who had been the cause of the poor cousin's death.

The Monkey on St. Laurenz.

St. Laurenz [1]) stood formerly where the revenue offices are now, and upon a little tower on that church, there was a monkey.

That monkey was the exact image of the one, which stole Emperor Ludwig den Bayer out of his cradle, and when they tried to take the little prince away from it, the monkey climbed upon the roof of St. Laurenz with the baby safe and sound.

It is not known what has become of the image.

But it would be a good thing if it could be found and put in the National Museum, where there are several other ancient relics from the church of St. Laurenz.

---

1) A tablet in the Alten Hof marks the spot where it stood.

St. Peter slants.

ealously guarded as St. Peter has always been, the top of the steeple bears witness to what once happened there. For there is no doubt, although the steeple itself is as straight as a candle, that the top slants a little.

Some think the reason is that it is not equally balanced, that the architect made a mistake, and talk in the way people generally do in these modern times, refusing to listen to myths or mysteries and trying to attribute a natural cause to everything, and if they cannot do that, believe nothing.

Others, more wisely, admit that something vital and inevitable, must have taken place there and offer various theories.

But when I was a child, I heard a tale from an old man, who had heard it from his grandfather, and although he may have told it in different words, it was about like this:

The city of Munich has always had beautiful churches, and as a rule it's people have always been so God-fearing, that formerly, it went by the name of the "German Rome". We had many friends, and only a few enemies, who called us as black as crows. Among our enemies was the Evil One, and his whole wicked pack. He had been longing, for many a year, to wring the necks of the good people of Munich, but as he could not do that, he vented his bad temper on churches and chapels.

He hated St. Peter above all other churches. For that church had always been the strong-hold of faith, and it's two steeples seemed to him like two fingers, which the city held up to heaven in token of eternal faith to God. Furthermore, the sound of the church bells irritated him, and when the sacred banner was hung out, he could hardly contain himself.

At last, he could stand it no longer, and went to work to destroy the church, or at least the two steeples. So, one midnight, he sent a fearful thunder-storm, and lightning struck the two steeples, and they caught fire and after swaying for a while, they fell. That was serious enough, for several buildings were buried under the ruins, and a number of people lost their lives, the towerkeeper being the first to meet his fate. Then the Evil One tried to destroy the church itself, but did not succeed in doing it any harm, because it was consecrated. The ridge-pole burnt a little when the lightning struck it, but the fire always went out. At that, the Evil One ceased from further attempt, and withdrew in the joy of victory, for he had satisfied his infernal craving, with the two steeples.

7*

It did not occur to anyone in Munich, that he was responsible for the misfortune; they attributed it to God's will, and a warning that they had failed in godliness, although neither the counsel or people and still less the clergy, knew wherein they had erred.

Then they began to consider whether they should build two steeples again, or only one, and decided upon the latter.

So a sketch was made of the future steeple, in which it had a roof ending in a point, and under the roof was an open gallery with an iron railing.

The towerkeeper could see everything, far and near, from that open gallery, and could give the alarm if there were a fire, or any signs of an enemy; and in times of peace, he and his assistant could go out upon the gallery, and play a sweet, sacred melody upon horns, from each of the four sides, to the delight and edification of all good Christians in Munich [1]).

When the Evil One saw that they were building up only one steeple again, he did not spend much thought upon it.

But when he became aware of all that was planned to take place on the top of the steeple, and especially the music of the horns, he fell into a rage again, for if the steeples had reminded him of an oath to God, this audible praise to Him was still more disagreeable.

When the steeple was at last finished, and on Saturday evening, the sacred music rang out over

1) The music still takes place on the evening before and morning of holidays, but there is no longer a watchman.

Munich, and the people gazed up at the steeple with delight and reverence, he decided to destroy that steeple just as he had the others.

Midnight approached, the sky was clear, the moon bright and full and everyone in the city was sleeping peacefully. At the stroke of twelve, the towerkeeper began his round upon the open gallery, and then he had a strange experience.

For suddenly there was a rushing, howling, whizzing, buzzing and dreadful roaring, and a hurricane struck the steeple of St. Peter, but nothing else, and it became pitch-dark. Keeper Heinz began to think of evil spirits, and in a minute, he was in no more doubt about it.

For he heard shrieking, laughing and blaspheming, and then he saw hideous forms flying toward the steeple, and the one nearest to him, no other than the Evil One himself, seemed to have the intention of pulling him over the railing, he grabbed and shrieked at him so horribly.

Upon that, the keeper rushed into his little room, and tearing the crucifix from the wall, he went out again under it's protection, and held the cross up before the other saying:

"What do you want? I am not afraid of you! Flee this place, at the sign of our Lord Christ!"

The devil started back under the spell of that name, and the hurricane abated a moment. But it began again immediately all the harder, and the whole pack crowded and pushed around the steeple; Satan, at the front, pressed on the railing, and as often as the keeper struck him on his horrid head with the cross, calling out, "Ha! Cursed spirit, I expel thee!" just so often the devil answered back: "Keep up your cursing and blows as long as you like! I spoiled two steeples for you, and shall do the same with this one! To-morrow you may tell them who did it!"

Shouted the keeper Heinz: "Ho! You eternally damned and wicked spirit, you will not succeed!"

And the devil: "Ho, yourself! Just wait until I show you and your eternally pious people of Munich! They will see what I can do!"

And then the battle up in the air, between the keeper, and Satan and his pack, began anew. The keeper felt the steeple rocking under him, and he could hardly hold the cross, his arm was so tired. At last there came a crash from above, as if the top of the steeple was falling apart, and he thought the end had come.

Just at that moment, though, it struck one, and instantly there arose an unspeakable shrieking and pushing and crowding around the roof of the steeple, until the stroke had entirely died away. Then with a swish and roar, all the horrid apparitions flew away from the steeple, the hurricane suddenly ceased, the darkness vanished, the sky became light and clear, the moon came out, and keeper Heinz fell upon his knees and gave thanks, in a loud voice, to God.

Early in the next morning, his assistant came as usual and could hardly believe the tale. But the other hurried down from the steeple, and went to the Rathhaus, letting a word fall here and there on the way, and he waked the priest, and then the burgomaster, and all the counsellors, and others as well. They listened to the keeper's story, and believed him as little as his assistant had done, because no one had heard the least noise; and discussing the matter thus, in all it's pros and cons, they sallied forth from the Rathhaus, and betook themselves to the market-place.

A crowd of people, who had already heard the reports, were standing about, and they were all staring up at the steeple, where one could see the keeper's assistant leaning over the railing, and looking up at the point of the steeple. When the priest, the beadle and the town counsellors, all did the same, they were greatly astonished, for the top of the steeple, which had been perfectly straight yesterday, was quite visibly aslant today!

There remained no further doubt as to the former steeples, for Heinz repeated every word. Everyone took comfort in the sign of God's protection and approval, for they considered that battle around the steeple of St. Peter, no proof of His displeasure, but rather of His love, and therefore their hearts were glad, and their resolve for enduring godliness was strengthened within them.

And they kept their resolve, for which reason no further mishap came to pass, and in the course of time, the top of the steeple righted itself considerably, but not entirely. It still slants a little, as a sign that no power can overturn our faith.

That was Anno sixteen hundred and eleven. It is possible too, it was twelve.

The Oriel Tower in the Old Courtyard.

ygone days and the people who lived in them, rise up before us, when we look at an old house, and especially one with an oriel window; it matters not whether we know their names or anything about them.

So much is certain; that joy and sorrow chased each other through those rooms, just as they do today, and always will, in the chequered accidents of this world.

The thought that those people were closely connected with the important events of their centuries, lends an especial background to fancy, and for that reason the eye lingers longer on such buildings than on modern ones. A great throng of people vanished from this world, is impressive in itself, and how much more so, when they were persons known to history, of high position in this world, often tasting more of bitterness than of sweetness, until, when their tasks were accomplished, they were allowed to go to their rest.

Such was often the case, in a similar house likewise with an oriel, namely in the old Ludwig's Burg at Munich.

The castle was begun by Duke Ludwig der Strenge and continued by his son, Emperor Ludwig der Bayer.

There is little doubt that the part with the oriel-tower was built first. The latter, with it's point above and below was considered a wonder at that time, and while no one ever came to Munich without going to see the tomb of Emperor Ludwig der Bayer, in the church of Unser Frauen, neither did anyone from far or near neglect a visit to Ludwig's Burg, to look at the little tower, about which the conundrum was put, "What points continually to heaven, and at the same time to earth, and although it's wings are bound fast, it has a flight?"

It is far from my purpose to make a parade of history here, but still I feel compelled to give a few hints about those who probably sat alone or with others, in the first storey or higher up, in that tower, chatting, or looking down into the courtyard. Many a delicate embroidery must have been wrought there, and many an old chronicle and legend read!

In all probability Duke Ludwig der Strenge, himself, lived there first, and the hapless Maria von Brabant, his first wife, whom he, in his unfounded jealousy, caused to be put to death at Donauwörth on the 18th of January, Ao. D. 1256.

It is still more probable that his second wife, Anna von Schlesien, and quite certain that his third, Mechtildis, daughter of Emperor Rudolph of Habsburg, lived there. Ludwig's sons and daughters all passed their youth, in what was built of the castle at that time.

In all likelihood, that son Ludwig, who was dispatched from life to death in a tournament at Nürnberg in Ao. 1290, by the lance of a çertain Count Grato von Hohenlohe; and in any case Rudolph, who after many quarrels with his brother Ludwig, left Bavaria only to die in a strange land; and Mechtilde who married and went to Lüneburg; Anna who married in Saxony, and another daughter whose name is uncertain, but about whom it is known that she entered a convent at Ulm.

All those right royal personages must have looked out often from the tower into the courtyard, where soldiers rattled in their armor, and court servants hurried to and fro, where counts and knights came riding in through the gate from Burgstrasse, or from the bare-footed monks on the other side, or when the counsellors or town judge came on this or that business. Bishops, abbots and clever monks were surely to be seen there from time to time, and a couple of court-fools running across the yard. The princes and young nobles probably practised their games, and fought their harmless duels there, the royal parents looking down at them from the oriel-tower. And when noon or vespers rang out from St. Laurenz opposite, or from the bare-footed monks, there was a pause in the chatting or reading, and the needle was stuck into the silk or velvet, while those in the oriel-window prayed devoutly together, or each for himself. Fancy it all! And many a time a troubadour stood there and sang old lore!

Taking the time, for instance, when the above-mentioned Ludwig was German Emperor, that noble prince must often have leaned by the window, or sat there in a merry mood, if the hour happened to be a happy one, and there were few enough of such in his life, or deep in thought if it were a time of danger or important crisis, as was usually the case. And at such a time, his first wife, the gentle Beatrix of Silesia was surely at his side murmuring words of comfort, and one or the other of their children, Mechtilde, Ludwig, Stephan or Agnes prattled at his knee.

And it was the same in the time of his second wife, Margarethe of Holland and Zealand, and their numerous children, namely, Ludwig, who was born in Rome and whose life was full of important events; and Wilhelm, who was Stadholder of Holland, and later, became hopelessly insane; furthermore Albert, to whom Straubing fell in the future division; then, Otto who became margrave and elector of Branden-burg; and the daughters, Margarethe and Elizabeth, and one little princess named Anna, who died when she was three years old, on a journey with her parents, and lies buried in the monastery of Castell.

After noble Emperor Ludwig's death, which occurred suddenly on the eleventh of October 1347, near the monastery of Fürstenfeld, which his father had founded as a penance for his dreadful sin toward Maria von Brabant, there followed many strange events and shifts of fortune, and various princes stood at the window in the oriel-tower; among them, that wild duke, Ludwig der Gebartete of Ingolstadt, who as you know, took the city away from his cousins, the dukes Ernst and Wilhelm, until they gained the power back again.

The same dukes, who later defeated him in the battle of Blutenburg, and drove him away for good. And then in the course of time, Duke Albert III stood at the window with Anna von Braunschweig, whom he had married some time after the murder of his beloved Agnes Bernauer, and Anna's children were probably there too; Johannes who died from the poisonous breath of the dragon which had flown into Munich; and Sigmund who founded the grand church of Unser Frauen, and who after his abdication, led a merry life in the little castle of Blutenburg; and their sister Margarethe who was married at Mantua; Albrecht, who was called the Wise, later; and strong Duke Christoph, he of many battles and adventures, who died at Rhodes; and Wolfgang who ruled Bavaria for three years, after Albrecht's death; and the fair Barbara who became a nun when she was still a girl, in the convent of St. Jacob on the Anger.

Add to all these, learned men of renown, and masters of painting and sculpture, who must have climbed the stairs to that little tower, to debate important questions with the princes, or to discuss an order they were to receive, to say nothing of the great commanders of the army, who may have cast a glance down into the courtyard, beginning at the time of Emperor Ludwig, and taking the hero, Seyfried

Schwepperman, as an instance, down to the time of Albrecht der Weise. When one thinks of all that, as one looks at that little oriel-tower, one must admit that we have still greater reason to consider it a symbol than those of yore.

All those princes and princesses have succumbed to the eternal law and lie in the earth on a level with all the others; the under point of the oriel symbolizes that; but we hope their souls have ascended to heaven, and spaces full of bliss.

As a symbol of their lives, the oriel tells us: Their wills would often have carried them higher, but their wings were bound to the earth, as the oriel is held by the firm wall upon which it strives to ascend.

And now you have a few hints about whom to meditate and dream, when you look up at the oriel-tower.

Concerning the Thievish Magpie, the Sunken Hands, the Emperor's Stone of St. Laurenz, Heinrich Barth, the Gustave Adolph Stone, the Marien Column, etc.

Enough has not been yet said about the magpie, on a certain house in Dienerstrasse[1]).

As I have already mentioned, a maidservant lived there, who was accused of having purloined jewels. She was condemned and suffered death, because everything testified against her. Afterwards it was discovered that a magpie had taken the gold and hidden it among the rafters of a neighboring house. That aroused much regret it is true, but it did not call the maid

---

1) It is on house no. 8 Residenzstrasse, which is the continuation of Dienerstrasse.

back to life, and so they had an image of the bird made, and put up to her memory, on the roof, over her little room.

I shall go into particulars about certain things in the cathedral of Unser Frauen later, but I wish to mention one, now; namely, the picture there, of a number of persons kneeling, and raising their folded hands, with the exception of one woman[1]).

There are different tales about that picture, but they all have the same starting-point, namely a will, which was misused, and by the aforesaid woman. One saying goes; the relatives were all praying together, when that woman's hands were suddenly lowered by an unseen power. Another is; they had suspected her for some time, but she nevertheless joined the others when they prayed for the departed, and nothing further happened. So their suspicions abated and when a large picture was painted in memory of the funeral services, the woman was included among the other relatives, and like them, her hands were folded and raised in prayer.

When the picture was hung and all those persons represented in it, met together to look at it, the woman was there also, and is supposed to have said; "I know that you suspect me of a great sin, but I forgive you for your lies; may God strike my hands down, if it was as you suspect!" She had scarcely uttered those words, the story goes, when the others looking at the picture, to hide their embarrassment, suddenly saw a change taking place in it, namely, the folded hands of the woman sank down.

---

1) In the second chapel at the left of the big door.

She was so frightened at that miracle, that she became speechless at first, and then fell very ill, and just before her death, she confessed that she had obtained her large share by fraud.

Everyone is free to choose whichever tale he prefers to believe.

Another old token is the Emperor's stone tablet which was formerly in the church of St. Laurenz near the old Burg, and after it had disappeared for a time, it was found and put up in the rectory of Unser Frauen, where it was little noticed until it was moved again to the Bavarian National Museum[1]). The relief represents Margarethe, the second wife of Emperor Ludwig der Bayer, holding the church of St. Laurenz; in the middle, is the holy Virgin Mary with the child Jesus, and the Emperor kneels on the other side, his hands folded reverently in prayer.

The gravestone or rather the bust of the old patrician Heinrich Barth, in the belfry of St. Peter is a token to us in Munich, of the marvellous and surpassing godliness, which characterized him and his four sons, who were the donors of the altar of the three kings.

Many houses in Munich, especially certain ones on Schrannenplatz[2]), were formerly painted with pictures, which were direct messages from forebears to their posterity. But unfortunately, they have been whitewashed over for the most part.

The meaning and significance of the sign of the three crowns is uncertain. Some consider it the sign of a

---

1) Raum 7.

2) Marienplatz was formerly called Schrannen or Marktplatz.

large inn, others, the token that ambassadors stayed in that house. There is a memorial tablet in Schrannenplatz[1]), by the way, saying that in Anno 1632, Gustave Adolphus of Sweden, stopped over night there.

The market-place will not be taken into further consideration at present, except to mention that splendid memorial column, which Elector Max I, Anno 1638, erected as a token of his thankfulness that Munich had escaped the fires and other calamities, with which so many places were visited, during the fearful Swedish war.

That memorial is the Marien column. Max only performed his solemn duty in commemorating the evil which had not happened. But many trials were still to come, and much horrible disaster followed. Munich, itself, which always seemed under God's especial protection, escaped, it is true, but Bavaria in general suffered.

However that may be, if Adolphus could come back here now, and see how well different religious beliefs exist side by side, and that the particular one which he tried to eradicate is still here, and if he should look out of his window and see the Marien column, it would furnish him with some material for serious thought.

A very remarkable fresco was to be seen up to the beginning of the 18th century, on the house on the corner of Fürstenfelderstrasse, which formerly belonged to the monastery of Ettal.

---

1) It was upon a house which was torn down to make way for the new Rathhaus.

The saying about it ran; Emperor Ludwig der Bayer was once in great embarrassment for money in Rome, and was accosted by an angel, some say by St. Benedict, who promised relief, if he would give freedom to a certain gentleman and his whole country, but above all if he would build a church and monastery, in honor of God and the Virgin Mary, on a certain spot in Bavaria.

When the Emperor had promised it all, the angel bestowed an alabaster image of the Virgin Mary, upon him, and vanished. Then the gentleman in question, really presented himself, and gave the Emperor a large sum of money, so that he was freed from all anxiety and could leave Italy. He founded the monastery above-mentioned, after a great many difficulties, because the particular place was not revealed to him, until an unknown hunter showed him the spot which was called Ampferang. That same Ampferang was a large mountain forest in the Ettika valley, and the name of the valley came from a proud Guelf prince, Ettiko, who was in great anger at his son who had given all his inherited lands over to the Carolingians, in order to receive them back increased in size, as fiefs. In his wrath, the old prince withdrew from the noise of the world, to the solitude of the mountains. That is the legend.

There are many other ingenious and clever theories about the name Ettal, some holding that the Emperor called it E-tal, the valley of the vow, the promise, and the new compact.

Be that as it may, Ettal monastery was built, and the Emperor continued to hold his court in

Ludwig's Burg; when it was partly destroyed by fire he moved into the house on the corner of Fürsten-felderstrasse, which belonged to him, and where he remained until the castle was repaired; then he returned to the castle and gave the house to the monastery, from which it received it's name.

The abbot caused a large picture to be painted upon it, as a memorial of gratitude, representing the Emperor receiving the alabaster Virgin, which he afterwards gave to the monastery church, from St. Benedict, who had appeared to him.

Such is the legend about the Ettal house and it's fresco. It is a pity that the latter was doomed to disappear. There are only a very few such pictures left in Munich; may they escape the whitewasher's brush!

St. Cajetan's Church.

any churches in Munich have some solemn vow to thank for their existence. That is also the case with St. Cajetan or the Theatiner church, and it is of especial interest for that reason, if for no other.

The story is as follows:

The great Elector Max I chose as bride for his electoral prince, Ferdinand Maria, the daughter of Victor Amadäus, Duke of Savoy, Adelheid Henrietta, whose picture so pleased the prince that he said yes, at once and gladly. Thereupon in October, Anno 1650, a brilliant embassy set off, the proposal was accepted, and on the 11th of December, the marriage by proxy took place in the cathedral of Turin. The real one with the electoral prince was postponed for some time, until after the death of Maximilian, Anno 1652, when

Adelheid left her native land with a large suite for Bavaria, entering Munich on the 22nd of June, and three days later, the wedding was celebrated with the new elector.

One could fill a small book, and possibly a large one, with accounts of the festivities, which took place before and after the wedding, and the merry-makings, as well as the people who were there. Then events full of importance to the kingdom followed, which by themselves would make an instructive and motley tale, and especially so, because after the death of the German Emperor, Ferdinand III, Ferdinand Maria of Bavaria, and the elector of the Palatinate, Carl Ludwig, disputed the regency of the empire, and so on. But all that is not in it's place here, as I am telling about the Theatiner church at Munich, not about the German empire.

In a word, though, everything turned out to the advantage and honor of Elector Ferdinand Maria, and according to his desire.

But one desire, alone, was unfulfilled by heaven.

No offspring had blessed his marriage and he longed for an heir.

Now Adelheid had already chosen a patron saint in Italy, namely St. Cajetan, a Count of Thiene by birth, who had gained much credit for himself by restoring and reforming the order of the Theatines. Those Theatine monks derived their name from the city Theats, or in Neapolitan, Chiati, where they were founded by Pope Paul IV.

In brief, Adelheid advised her husband to make a vow to St. Cajetan, that he would introduce his order into Munich and build a fine monastery and a beautiful church for them.

Not long after Elector Ferdinand Maria had made the vow, he was blessed with a little princess; that was excellent in it's way, but he had wanted a prince. When Adelheid, some time after, was looking forward to another happy event, she felt so sure of the result, that she told Ferdinand his wish was about to be fulfilled by heaven, and that he must make the necessary plans for the monastery and church, and write to Augustinus Bozomo, the general of the Theatines, to send some regular clergy and novices to Munich.

That was done accordingly, and behold! Before the corner-stone for the church and monastery was laid, Ferdinand Maria possessed a little electoral prince, Max Emanuel, who in later years was not so fond of peace and quiet as his illustrious father.

The corner-stone was laid, however, on April 29th 1652.

Since there is so little learning in this book I will insert a few latin lines, namely, that which was engraved upon a golden tablet and laid on the corner-stone; it ran as follows:

Auspice. D. O. M.
In honorem S. Adelaidis Imperatricis
et Divi Cajetani Thienaei
Ferdinandus Maria Elector
Utr. Bavar. Dux etc.
et
Henrietta Maria Adelais
Princeps Regalis Sabaudiae
Ejus Uxor

Ecclesiam hanc cum adjuncta Domo
Patribus Clericis Regularibus
fundaverunt
Et primum lapidem posuerunt
Anno orbe redempto
MDCLXIII
Die XXIX Aprilis.

Then the Italian architect Augustin Barella, who was given the work, began to build with right good courage. The monastery was finished in a short time, but it was Anno 1675, the 11th of July, before the church was dedicated by the Freising bishop, Johannes Kühner.

In the church there are many details of importance such as the Lauretan chapel, the chapel of the Holy Grave, and holy stairs, like those at Rome.

I would like to give an accurate description of that splendid, and still, in so many respects, home-like church, but it would fill too much space; moreover, that above-mentioned knight of St. Lazarus and syndic, Anthoni Wilhelmus Ertel, has taken the best part away from me, in his aforesaid "Bavarian Atlantis" where he says: "It has three small doors on each side, and windows over the chapels, and in the middle of the church, a cupola swings itself up, high into the air, comely and full of light, decorated with the finest pictures and with fruits made of plaster. There are altars all around the church painted by the most excellent artists, among which the brush of the famous Sandrart shines forth, as well as many works of art by Italians."

You will hear more about the Electress Adelheid and her order, at another time.

Since it has been mentioned who are buried in the crypts of other churches, that of Theatiner church should not be omitted.

A little son and daughter of the founder, were first laid to rest there; then Ao. 1667, on the 18th of March, Adelheid of Savoy; later Ao. 1679, on the 26th of May, Elector Ferdinand Maria.

Their eldest daughter, Maria Anna Christina Victoria who was married in France, lies buried in the royal graves at St. Denis, not far from Paris. But the renowned and eldest son, Max Emanuel, was laid in the crypt at Munich, after his many battles, hopes and disappointments.

Obiit Ao. 1726, the 27th of February, between 7 and 8 o'clock.

His first wife was Maria Antonia Josepha Benedicta Rosalia Petronella, daughter of Emperor Leopold. She died in Vienna and is buried there. A son by that marriage, prince Joseph, who had a number of other names as well, is buried in Brussels. He is the same who was named heir of the Spanish monarchy. Elector Max Emanuel's second beautiful wife, Theresia Kunegunde Sobieska of Poland, died in a foreign country also, at Venice. Some of their children are in the crypt at Munich, but others are not, for instance Phillip Moritz Maria Dominikus Joseph died at Rome where he was about to be made a bishop, and Clemens August, who became Elector of Cologne, lies in the cathedral there.

Max Emanuel was succeeded by his son, Carl

Albrecht, as German Emperor, Carl VII. His wife Maria Amalia, Emperor Joseph's daughter, rests near him.

Then came the much loved Elector Max III, with whom, Ao. 1777, the Ludwig line died out, and the descendants of Rudolph, Emperor Ludwig's brother, succeeded to the throne.

Elector Karl Theodor was the first.

He was followed by King Max Joseph I, at whose name, all Bavarians are filled with deep emotion.

The Hunger Bell in Theatine Monastery and the Theatine Clock.

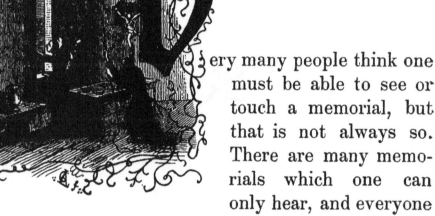

Very many people think one must be able to see or touch a memorial, but that is not always so. There are many memorials which one can only hear, and everyone knows what they mean and what he ought to do, but does not always do it.

How is it with the prayer, when mid-day or Ave Maria rings?

But I must tell about the ringing of another bell, namely the hunger bell of St. Cajetan.

As you already know, Elector Ferdinand Maria called the Theatine monks to Munich. They were especially commanded by the reformer of their order, to live from alms alone, but they could not beg, and must wait until provisions came to them at the will of heaven. And only when those provisions were too long in coming, and three days of fasting had passed, were they justified in pulling a certain bell, to let the outside world know of their unfortunate situation.

That was certainly no more than proper and just, for having nothing at all, is going rather far, even for the greatest abstemiousness.

Firmly as the Theatines were resolved to live in poverty, just so firmly did they rely upon their hunger bell, in case of need. But they had no cause for a long time to make use of it, because the princely founder of the monastery, and his successors, took care that they received what was necessary.

That became such a habit, that other people in Munich bethought themselves less and less about exercising the same charity, because they knew the good Theatine monks had enough to live on.

That being the case, and no one suspecting any evil, it was a great surprise to hear a bell suddenly begin to ring, on St. Peter's day in 1727. It was a bell which had never been heard before, and it did not ring and then stop, like other bells, but kept on as if it never meant to end.

People collected and stood about in groups, talking, and at last hit upon the idea, that the loud and clear tones came from the hunger bell of St. Cajetan, and when it began to stop, and only a few more disjointed strokes were heard, some thought the lay-brother who was ringing, was so exhausted by hunger that he had not the strength to pull longer on the rope.

At that, every one started in haste to bring help to the Theatines: and in a short time, bread, chickens, fruit, veal and fish, barley-water and other drinks, were there in abundance, and wood, also, to cook with. Supplies from the electoral court-kitchen were there before all the others, and so the Theatines were not only rescued for the moment, from their desperate position, but they could consider themselves in supplies for a few weeks ahead, for which they were correspondingly thankful.

That unfortunate state of things had come about thus; the court-cook, Kornet, had been attacked by shooting pains in his limbs, as was often the case and had gone to bed, forgetting in his *dolores* to remind his substitute Heinsler junior, that the customary time had come for sending supplies to the Theatines. They say he made all sorts of apologies in the monastery afterwards, and received the answer; "It was of no importance, for although the danger seemed great at first, and otherwise they would not have rung the bell, it had passed, and the end was much better than they could have dreamed".

That was the way it happened once, and fifteen years later, it happened again. But that was the last time, and it was quite enough, for although three is a lucky number, two famines are enough.

Although the tale about the hunger bell is probably correct, I cannot aver the same about the Theatine clock, and the saying attached to it, although chance once or twice has made it appear true.

The saying is that when the Theatine clock runs down, a death occurs very soon in the Bavarian royal house.

At any rate the clock has run down several times

to my knowledge, and I never heard of any death following, which could cause especial mourning in the ruling house or in the land of Bavaria.

There was a much earlier saying, that it was a bad omen if the clock of the cathedral struck too many times.

It may be so, and it may not, I cannot commit myself.

The Turkish Flag and Tent in the Cathedral of Unser Frauen, and the Turkish Ditch, and Cardinal's Hat in the Air.

ach of the two relics mentioned first, dates from the victories of Elector Max Emanuel over the Turks, in Hungary.

The flag may be seen at any time in the cathedral[1]), and the tent, or rather, the top of it, is carried in the Corpus Domini procession.

The long deep ditch outside Munich, dates from the same time of victory; Elector Max Emanuel purposed bringing a canal by that means to Munich, and employed a large number of Turkish prisoners in digging it.

---

1) In the nave, hanging from a pillar.

The memorial of an ecclesiastic, namely a cardinal's hat, hung suspended in mid-air over the choir[1]) of Unser Frauen, until a few years ago. It was in memory of Cardinal Melchior Clessel, Bishop of Vienna, and held by most to have been the son of a baker of Munich. The severely-tried Clessel, who was as distinguished a statesman as prince of the church and priest, came to Munich once, where he paid particular honor to the relics of St. Benno, and left the aforesaid token of remembrance, besides many valuable church ornaments.

When the cathedral was being restored, the hat was removed and put in the sacristy.

You will read later of many other interesting things in the cathedral of Unser Frauen.

---

1) Now in the fourth chapel on the right from the big door.

Concerning Ghosts and Apparitions in Munich.

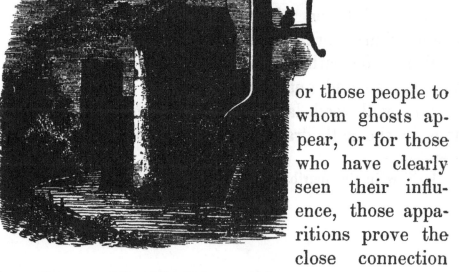

For those people to whom ghosts appear, or for those who have clearly seen their influence, those apparitions prove the close connection of another world with this earthly one.

Hence I am going to tell about ghosts and apparitions in Munich, even if some of you are so enlightened as to take umbrage at it.

The church of Heiligen Geist is in the Thal at Munich.

At the very first, it was called St. Catherine's chapel, and Duke Ludwig, the Kelheimer, added a pilgrim's house to it, which his son, Otto, rebuilt into a large hospital.

Not far behind it, was the graveyard. And there at midnight of St. John's day, they say unpleasant things happened; the graves opened letting out a procession of pilgrims and invalids, "who behaved in an unseemly and nowise grateful way, showing more inclination to eat and drink, than to pray out of their psalters".

And in the neighborhood of the house with the picture in Westenriederstrasse, strange things happen even now, they say.

If one goes through the court-house[1]) into the passage inside, one can see through a window into the ancient garden of the Augustines and the cloister, in a part of which one is standing at the moment, only it has all been changed.

There are strange stories about that little garden.

I will relate one which used to be told me in my youth by a reliable person, namely, an old man whose father was closely connected with it.

His father, so he was wont to begin, was a leech, and was often called to the Augustine monastery. That happened once in the middle of the night, when a certain corpulent and pious friar had such a rush of blood to the head, that bleeding was ordered. As the aforesaid father and leech was passing through the lower cloister, he glanced in at the door of the little garden which strangely enough was ajar, and there he saw an Augustine monk, who had been dead for a long time, appear and say "Pray for me!" and then disappear again.

The leech, his father, was seized by no small

---

1) The old Augustine monastery at the right of St. Michaels on Ettstrasse.

fright at that, and although he was able to bleed the friar, he had an attack of chills and fever afterwards which took three months to cure. But he carried out the wish of the Augustine, and although he passed that door often and at all hours in the course of time, he never saw it ajar again, and nothing ever happened to him a second time, for without doubt his devout prayers had been accepted.

I used also to hear tales about the Duke Maxburg, when I was a boy.

The Electress Marianne is supposed to haunt the castle, but in a mild and gentle form. In spite of her harmlessness, though, everyone who sees her is thrown into a panic, and one winter night a sentry who had taken to flight, fell down senseless in the deep snow in the little courtyard outside, where he remained until the next morning, entirely covered by the snow. The night-sentry who came to relieve guard and found no one there, did not know what to think. He looked everywhere and inquired of everyone but no explanation was to be found: the guard of the gate said he had seen no one, and the matter remained a puzzle until toward morning. The snow began to blow around then, and two legs came to light, upon which they pulled out the rest of the sentry.

Fortunately he was still alive, but they say, a little more, and he would have been totally frozen. And that would have been no trifle for he was not only a soldier, but the father of a family, having a lawful wife and two living children, who would have suffered a great loss.

Naturally, they were joyful enough, to hear that the danger was over.

The people who came by, were all so charitable, that in a short time enough money had been collected to enable the soldier to indulge in a warm nourishing breakfast and a glass of wine.

The Capuchin friars whose little monastery was near the castle, would not allow that however, but took him in, and treated him to all sorts of good things, whereupon he did not ask for more soup, but he did ask for a glass of "brown" more than three times, because he still felt cold in this or that part of his body, until at last he was warm and comfortable all over; then he gave thanks and went out, and told the people there about his strange experience of lying in the snow. After that, he went home with his wife, and two children, taking the money with him and followed by a crowd of people.

That man was named Johannes Steindl and it happened at the beginning of the nineties.

It is so well known that there were rappings in the large corner house on the left of Schleckerstrasse only a few years ago, that nothing more need be said about it. There is no more rapping there now, it is true, but I do not wish to vow for anything.

There is no doubt, however, that in the corner house near the Rathhaus in Burgstrasse, a ghost appears now sometimes, at midnight, all in white, with a bald head, and looks down into the street. It is the ghost of the wicked lawyer, Dr. Calomälus, who lost his wig in Starnberg lake, after he had got people to quarrelling with each other. I have written up the whole affair, in my "Guten Alten Zeiten".

The Jungfern Tower[1]) was just around the corner near the Greek market-place.

It was haunted too, and at times one could hear groans and a rattling of chains from below; and several people who had lost their way, at different times, say they saw a figure with a large three-cornered hat and a queue, who rang his hands and disappeared again.

Without doubt that ghost was responsible for many an imprisonment if not for worse.

The right hand steeple of Unser Frauen is also supposed to be haunted, and sometimes one hears a most startling croaking, wheezing and cackling there. Some people think it is night-owls. It may be, but there is also a chance that it is not night-owls.

Things are not quite right in the city armory either, for several times a suit of armor has moved about, and formerly in the big garret of the old castle, strange things happened among the old chests, wrought-iron etc.

Now, far be it from me to affirm that the Wandering Jew was a ghost for according to all reports, he often appeared in a substantial and tangible form, in different places in Germany.

But at the same time he did not belong to this world because he ought to have been dead for a long time, if heaven had permitted him to die.

_____

1) A tablet on the remnant of old city wall marks the spot where the tower was.

Perhaps he really is dead now, for since the beginning of the last century, nothing has been seen or heard of him either in any part of the kingdom, or here at Munich.

At that time, Ao. 1702, he came as usual from the direction of the Salzburg highway to the Gasteig and wanted to go into Munich. But they prevented him. He took that meekly and said to the people standing about that the picture of Christ on the little hill there, was a perfect likeness of the Saviour, and he prayed for a long time on the little bench before it, and after he had distributed beads and rosaries among the crowd, old and young, he went away again.

Another ominous apparition was the mourning-woman of Augsburg, who haunted Munich at one time.

Those who have looked the matter up, have come to this that and the other conclusion, no two alike. But they agree in so far that the mourning-woman took the new-born child of a rich Munich burgher's wife, who had been confined in Augsburg, and put another one in it's place. It was discovered and the burgher's wife died from grief as well as the two babies. The curse of God rested upon the robber from that time forth, and she died without the last communion, and found no rest in the grave, but kept going to Munich, where she appeared wherever a child was in danger of death.

I have told nearly enough about these melancholy apparitions now, and shall mention only one more of which I heard tales in my youth. It concerns the

Noah's Ark [1]) beer-garden of olden times in Wurzerstrasse. On the one side, a narrow flight of stairs
led down to the beer-garden with it's big trees, which
we all remember, and when one had imbibed his
"brown", he could go back the same way, and it was
usually with a much heavier head than he had brought
with him, or he could leave by some other narrow
stairs, on the side toward the Hofgarten.

The beer-garden in question was especially popular
among the electoral Leibhartschiere [2]), when their services in the Residenz were not needed, and they are
said to have shown almost as great devotion to Noah's
Ark as they have always shown for their duty.

Once they had arranged an especial festivity for
the name-day of one of their comrades, Eberhard
Häcker, and the latter had been released from duty
for that evening. During the two weeks, which elap-
sed before the appointed time came, however, the guest
of honor died.

When his comrades and friends had assembled
in the Noah's Ark upon the evening they had originally planned, and were gravely drinking their "browns"
and the hour had become a late one, someone said;
"It was a sad pity, that their dear comrade could not
have been there for his festival. But now he was
free from guard duty and all earthly annoyances of
that sort, and had received a proof of their friendship.
So he proposed, though the time was more than up,

1) It was between Wurzer and Marstallstrasse — not far
behind Hotel Vier Jahreszeiten.
2) Body guard archers.

to have their mugs filled once more, and drink to the honor of their dead comrade."

All the other Hartschiere and friends were agreed to that, although more than one had already risen to put his high, round hat upon his head, with it's demure looking queue.

When the mugs had been filled again, and they had emptied them, standing, in honor of their dead comrade, the former speaker said, "That would surely have tasted good to our departed friend, if he had only been here." They all nodded their heads in solemn silence, when suddenly they heard two deep sighs, coming from Wurzerstrasse above.

Naturally the Hartschiere were not a little startled and turned all at once toward the narrow stairs, and there on the top step they saw their dead friend, as natural as life, looking dolefully down at them. Then he raised his right hand slowly, saluted them, and sighed a third time. After that, he seemed to turn into a sort of light, which gradually disappeared. As one might expect, all that made such an impression upon the live Hartschiere, that they stood there like blocks of stone, and although the nearest way home for most of them was by that little flight of stairs, every man of them chose those near the Hofgarten later, and went home by a round-about way.

Those who had that experience in the nineties, saw no reason to make a secret of it, so the story spread abroad. I asked old Wendelin who was in service at the time, about it, and he made short work of all my arguments, saying he could not deny what he had seen with his own eyes. I made further inquiries of a certain Hartschier who had known Häcker and he said, "He himself had not been present on that occasion in the nineties, but it was unquestionably true, that that same Häcker had been seen again several times, and once when he was there; so there could be no doubt about it."

So much for Noah's Ark.

Lastly, a few words about the city-angel.

Upon the occasion of the seven hundredth anniversary of the city of Munich, I wrote a little book, called "Münchner Geister", wherein one can see that I, myself, have looked upon and talked with him, half dreaming, half waking.

In case some of you have not read the book, I will give a very brief account of what the spirit is like.

In the first place, he is a benevolent spirit and beautiful of face. A good deed gives him the greatest joy. He watches over good people and sees to it, that too heavy and numerous difficulties do not block their way, and brings it about that hard, stern judgments become milder just at the right moment, and so on. As he serves good people by bringing about happy chances for them, so does he inspire useful ideas in them, and on name-festivals and Christmas, he who receives a present, does not have to guess long from whom it came, for it is either from the city-angel directly, or from someone to whom he whispered the act of love.

But on the other hand he is all the more severe with bad people, and plays all sorts of pranks upon them; he leads them on the most round-about ways,

so that they arrive too late for their wicked enter-
prises, or they do not find the persons or objects upon
which they have designs, and his ingenuity in catching
the wicked in their own traps, is marvellous.

Then again, he is full of pity for the fallen; when
someone is imprisoned and half out of his mind, the
city-angel goes to him invisibly, or in the visible form
of some kindly person, and whispers to the prisoner
to mend his ways, and take comfort.

He is very rigorous, when he comes across real
callousness, however, and if the scoundrel tries to
escape, he puts every possible impediment in his way,
so that he is caught in spite of all his wiles and
cunning. When he sees that confidence has been
betrayed, or propriety or morals sinned against, being
always on the particular lookout for listeners, then
he throws mildness to the winds, and gives the sinner
a slap in the face, which he does not quickly forget,
as a little reminder of a higher justice.

Formerly one heard of remarkable instances where
no one but the city-angel could possibly have been
concerned. It was he who made the tongue of a
slanderous girl, whirl around like a little wheel, until
she bitterly repented; then the tongue went slower
and slower and finally stopped.

In the time of Duke Sigmund, a certain man was
in great trouble, and did not dare go to the castle
about it, because one of the court servants was his
bitter enemy, and would have seen to it that he did
not get what he wished; so one evening he had given
up all hope, and was wandering about in the wind
and snowdrifts. Then it seemed to him as if he heard

someone saying, "Go into that hall-way". He did so, and shortly after, another person entered, and as soon as the latter spoke the man recognized the Duke.

Then he told his trouble and was listened to. That same evening, the court servant, after receiving a sound scolding, had to bring him the money which the Duke had granted him. The city-angel had brought it all about.

When Hans Steininger, the learned and clever Braunau counsellor, with the celebrated beard which reached to his feet, whose portrait hangs on the stair-case of the Residenz, when that same Steininger came to Munich to the Neuveste and stared too much at a pretty chambermaid, although he had a good wife of his own at home, he stumbled suddenly over his own beard, and but a little more, would have fallen down stairs.

That was the city-angel again.

And likewise in Burgstrasse at Schneeberg on the Sonnen corner. In that house, the dentist, Naras, was complaining about the bad times, saying, "Good Lord! Is there no one with a toothache any more?" when he was seized with a severe one himself.

That was the city-angel's joke.

And it was he who egged the two jealous hunch-backs, Merlin and Kimmerle, tailors to the Dukes Wilhelm and Ferdinand, on to each other, until they fought with swords in the courtyard one day, and were shut up in the same prison cell, for it. They continued to fight there and their time of punishment was extended a day each time. At last they made it up and remained friends after that.

He played pranks on the doctors especially Dr. Golzius in the Thal, who was in the habit of eating everything he forbade his patients, and of making jokes about it. Once when Duke Wilhelm IV had sent him a fish, he had such a terrible pain in the stomach that he did not feel inclined to make any more jokes.

In short, one was never safe from the city-angel, and is not now, and getting into his bad graces is no comfortable experience.

St. Benno.

I have already mentioned that St. Benno is the patron saint of Bavaria, and therefore his memory is especially honored.

Any one who wishes to read a detailed account of the fine old bishop of Meissen, will find it in my "Plauder-Stüblein", and how his relics were solemnly transferred to Munich, Ao. D. 1576, after having been moved from place to place, as if there was no rest in the grave for the saint.

And of especial note is, that the relics of the holy Bishop Benno were preserved in the chapel of the ducal castle for four years after their arrival, before they were moved to the cathedral of Unser Frauen, where an especial altar was erected for them, with a picture recording his miracles, and where his mitre, dalmatic and staff are to be seen[1]). In the

1) The fifth chapel on the left from the big door.

same chapel are statues of two princes, Ignatius and Hieronimus, who dedicated themselves to him, and recovered thereby from illness. And lastly, one must not forget the little Benno-fountain, which is outside the church near the sacristy, the water of which is supposed to cure certain diseases of the eye.

Concerning Various Reminiscences of Old Munich.

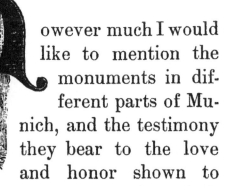

owever much I would like to mention the monuments in different parts of Munich, and the testimony they bear to the love and honor shown to Bavaria, lack of space prevents me; besides that, their meaning and value are very plain.

But there are many other instances in which that is not the case, so I will call my reader's attention to these, and try to make their significance clearer than a passing glance reveals. I have often noticed, for example, that many people do not know what the banners of handicrafts really mean, which are carried in religious processions, notably in that of Corpus Domini.

It is in this wise:

Formerly the master of a craft and his assistants went to war when the safety of the city or of the dukes demanded it, and each little group had it's own small banner. Later, when military service was performed by soldiers alone, the citizens did not wish their own bravery to be entirely forgotten, and as a token of it for their descendants, they changed the small banners into large flags and standards, with the picture of some saint and the name of a craft, with this or that mark of honor which the dukes, or emperor himself, had conferred upon it.

Mention should be made first of the standard of the weavers and particularly of the old sword and battle-axes which are carried in the Corpus Domini procession. The latter date from the year 1422, and were taken with many other weapons from the men of Duke Ludwig der Gebartete, in the battle of Blutenburg, when he was trying to take Munich again. According to other accounts, the sword and battle-axes were taken from Ludwig's men much earlier, in the time of the wicked burgomaster, when the ducal cousin made a triumphal march through Anger Gate into the Zwinger, and the weavers who had remained faithful to the two dukes through it all, wrested them from his men. But I cannot quite believe that, because the ducal cousin would never have allowed an act like that to go unpunished, and we have no account of any such punishment, and besides, in that case, the weapons would surely have been lost.

So I hold to the opinion that the sword and axes of the weavers date from the battle of Blutenburg and that the weavers received them as a reward from the dukes to whom they rendered distinguished service in the battles of Blutenburg, Alling, and Hoflach especially in freeing Duke Ernst's son Albrecht from the hands of the enemy, just as later they received the right to carry the imperial eagle upon their banner from Emperor Siegmund.

The privilege of carrying the city coat-of-arms, if not the imperial eagle, had already been given several crafts, for instance, the shoemakers.

That dates from Ao. 1295 when Ludwig der Bayer, later Roman Emperor, was being educated at the imperial court of Vienna, and his elder brother, Rudolph, was living at Munich.

A serious dispute arose between that same Rudolph and Wolfart, bishop of Augsburg. The latter had destroyed the castle of Kaltenberg on the Paar river, and at that Rudolph sent out his field-marshal to seize Margarethen, or Mergethen, castle. The people of Augsburg wanted to get that back again and did not succeed, and a general burning and devastating now in Bavaria now in Swabia, followed. All the little banners were destroyed in the battle of Mergethen, which the Bavarians and Augsburgers fought before the castle itself, for although the Bavarians fought from within the castle, of which they had gained possession, they had hard work in forcing the enemy back, and were overcome at last; one banner alone, that of the shoemaker guild was saved. Later, they received as a reward from Emperor Ludwig der Bayer, the right to the city coat-of-arms, and the permission to celebrate their anniversary day in St. Laurenz church near Ludwig's castle.

Emperor Ludwig der Bayer rewarded the guild of bakers for their bravery and devotion in the battle of the Two Emperors, Ao. 1322, by giving them the imperial eagle and something else. The latter exists today [1]), although it's purpose has been changed. Namely the Emperor built a little house for them in the Thal, on the left coming from the town-hall over High Bridge, in which house some old and decrepit baker was to be taken care of; and he also granted them a fraternity.

That support was offered in the little house, from then on, up to the beginning of the nineteenth century when the house was sold and the baker home removed to another, where some old baker continued to live in comfort.

After the sale of the little house of the baker fraternity, the pictures and inscriptions upon it were whitewashed over.

If anyone cared to remove that wash, the following would come to light.

In the first place a picture, in which the emperor gives a title-deed to the bakers; above it was the imperial eagle which also ornamented the vessels of the fraternity, which were used in church services.

And in the second place, three long verses would partially appear.

Under the picture was written:

"Emperor Ludwig, that true hero
A chosen prince of Bavaria,

1) No trace of the house remains, but a tablet on the corner of Hochbrückenstrasse and the Thal, shows where it stood.

Conferred upon the baker guild,
A writ of mighty power.
Because of their brave act
His imperial majesty
In the battle rescuing, .
The house he gave them, as a gift.
And upon their banner,
The eagle is emblazoned.
In old lore, it is written,
Of bakers there were five,
Who started this fraternity.
God give the brothers and sisters peace!"

On the left side was the following;

"When one reckoned one thousand
Three hundred and three (two) and twenty
After Christ's birth and the chosen one
The true hero was ruling,
Emperor Ludwig manifestedly,
Duke Friedrich of Austria
Marched against him, strong
In a great army's might,
And in Milldorf was the battle.
Fate hung over the Emperor.
When the bakers saw it all
They drew up around the Emperor
And with their weapons
Drove back the Austrian horde,
And saved the Emperor
To win the battle gloriously,
So the Emperor gave them as a sign.
The eagle on their banner,
And fortified with rightful law
The fraternity of Our Lady.
And furthermore he built for them
A house at München in the Thal
Hard on the Hofbruck mill near by.
God grant the Emperor eternal peace
Is the brothers' and sisters' earnest wish."

On the right was written;

    "When one counted one thousand three
    Hundred years and two and twenty
    That had passed since birth of Christ,
    The town was small and sparse
    And on this spot a linden fine,
    Where the baker brothers
    Often held their gatherings
    And carried out their plan
    Of starting a fraternity
    In honor of Our Lady.
    The matter was discussed
    And laid before the Emperor,
    Who when he saw their wish
    Agreed to it most willingly
    For he held them high.
    Because he honored them so high,
    Since they had saved him in the battle,
    From threatening danger,
    He thought to add to his one favor,
    And caused a small house to be built.
    And gave his signature and seal.
    Besides he honored them with permission,
    To carry the imperial eagle,
    A favor no craft had ever had,
    However sharp and clever.
    And so the fraternity did build
    In praise of God and of
    Our Lady.
    And after that, increased so far
    As three hundred counties and towns."

So ran the inscriptions under the whitewash. The mode of speech and much else, particularly the four last lines, indicate that they were not put upon the house when it was first built, but much later, for how could they tell in the beginning that three hundred cities and towns would join them.

In all probability the baker fraternity applied, later, to a renowned school-teacher and master of poets in Munich, very likely about Ao. 1500 and begged him to mount his Pegasus, and bring them something worth having from Olympus, — which he evidently did — and after he had composed the three poems, they were painted upon the house together with the pictures, that is my opinion.

I would like to have been there when the master read his rhymes for the first time to the bakers, and after the whole composition was inscribed upon the wall, I would like to have seen him going around outside the city so that he could come in at Isar Gate, apparently quite by chance, and passing the little house, glance up at his verses, saying to himself; "I composed all that, and it will stay up there for eternity".

And when he found others standing there looking up at the house, his heart must have swelled with pride.

I can easily fancy it, and how the schoolmaster in his quiet joy, turned aside by way of the High Bridge through Thalbrucken Gate and Wein Stadel over the market-place to Weinstrasse, then on the left into Sporer alley and around the back side of the cathedral past the sacristan's house[1]) to the small house at the right where a very short alley leads to Schäfflerstrasse.

That schoolmaster and poet probably lived in the small house, for in it was the celebrated poet-school

---

1) No. 11 Frauenplatz.

of the ducal city of Munich, and there is little doubt that the poet of Nürnberg, Hans Sachs, lived there when he visited us after his wanderings in France, very likely on his way home.

Be that as it may, the aforesaid poet-school, in which sons of rich citizens received instruction, was also the residence of the master, who before receiving the position, was obliged to prove himself as good a poet, as the towerkeepers good trumpeters. At any rate the house is worth looking at if only in remembrance of that one schoolmaster and his kindly rhymes, to say nothing of all his colleagues, who sooner or later made names for themselves, and who probably understood playing the lyre as well as swinging the rod.

Later there was a change in the poet's house when the number of pupils had increased, so that it was built out as far as the sacristan's house, and after the school had been moved elsewhere quite different people lived in it.

Speaking of the poet-and school-house, reminds me of a certain good widow who lived there later, in the part next the sacristan's house in the room with the large window.

The woman's name was Petronella Stromair, and as her husband had left her riches, although she was far advanced in years, there were two men, as often happens in such cases, who tried to convince her she ought to marry again, assuring her they had no thought of her money but only wanted her, herself.

Now, widow Petronella Stromair had insight enough to take such statements exactly reversed, and seeing that they were ready to make a fool of her, she determined to give them both a lesson, so she said to each, taking care that neither knew anything of the other's intentions;

"She must have time to think about it, and if they granted three requests she had to make, she hoped all would end satisfactorily. The first request, however, was peremptory and as follows; she must have a year to think about it and at the end of that time they must come back and ask again."

As there was nothing to do but to comply with the request, they stayed away, and at the expiration of the time, presented themselves again, each separately, on two different, appointed days.

They were not a little astonished when the worthy widow said she had almost decided but not quite, and her second urgent request was that they stay away a second year and then come and ask again, and she added to the second suitor, "as far as she knew a serious obstacle would be removed for him by that time."

She said that, because she saw from the behavior of the first suitor that he probably would not come back a second time.

That proved to be the case too, for a year later, only the second came back.

When he asked what she had decided, she said that two thirds of her decision was made, but her third request was that he give her still another year for consideration, and then she would have a definite answer for him; in the meantime she could tell him, however, that the serious obstacle, she had spoken of, had been removed, and that fact would help him greatly in attaining his end.

When her lover, or rather the lover of her money, asked what the obstacle had been, she said:

"He had had a rival who had not stood the test and the only reason she could think of was that he had probably suspected she was going to put him off a second and then a third time as she had nominally done the first time. She hoped he who had come a second time would not show such scepticism as to believe that she who was now two years more advanced in age could act with such slyness, just as she on her side believed she was not loved on account of her money, in spite of her great age. But at the same time, she would be very thankful to hear him solemnly swear to the latter, and if he could do that she might possibly let him off from the third year and marry him at once!"

After the suitor had sworn to it by all that was sacred and holy, she said;

"He had made her very happy, she was ready now to fulfil his wishes, and first she would give him an idea of what she possessed, and of her last will and testament, for it was always best to be prepared for what might happen, and if he were satisfied with it she would have it signed before him by a couple of witnesses, and closed and sealed, and given into a lawyer's keeping."

Thereupon she went to a chest and taking out a paper, gave it to the suitor, who took it with ill-concealed eagerness and began to read.

The first page which consisted of an inventory

of her property, seemed to make a very good impression upon him, and, with a word of praise for her thrift, he turned the page full of happy expectations.

But after turning the page so serenely, he became suddenly agitated, and his face turned from red to white — for he had read that he was not the heir, but that half went to a faithful old serving-woman, and the other half to the poor of Nürnberg which was her native city.

"Why do you tremble and stare so?" she asked, "Do you not like it that I have left my property to others instead of to you? You want only me, not my money!"

"Oh just so, just so, only you", stammered the rascal, "and I offer you a proof of it! I will give you the year's time you asked for, and then I will come back! That is, I would like to take you at your word now, very gladly, but I have a journey to make, which prevents me, just at this moment, from — from entering into the — the bonds of matrimony." "In that case I will not insist or hinder you" said Frau Petronella Stromair, "farewell, and if we do not meet again here, then may it be in a better world."

The rogue bowed low, and murmuring all sorts of promises, he departed, and did not return on the appointed day, the third year.

Petronella Stromair had expected as much and was in nowise disturbed by it. On the contrary, she was full of quiet satisfaction at having played her game so well with the two designing fellows, and as she told the story to one or two of her relatives, it soon became generally known.

Petronella lived a full half dozen years after that, and Ao. 1601, she passed away in the Lord, and was buried diagonally opposite her dwelling, where one may still see her black tombstone lying sideways, on the sacristy wall. She is portrayed upon the stone, and although it is much damaged by time, one may still see from her face that she was one of the right sort.

So much for Petronella Stromair. Near by, on the same wall of the sacristy, is a gravestone with an epitaph in high relief, which is said to have been the incentive to lithography.

The little fountain exactly opposite the former school of poets, is a memorial of a religious character. It was erected in honor of St. Benno, of whom I have already spoken, and it's waters are supposed to cure many diseases of the eye.

In regard to the gravestones on the walls of Unser Lieb Frauen, many a one preaches sermons for those who have ears to hear, and I can assure you that such is particularly the case with the most dilapidated ones, about each of which, a small book could be written.

I cannot go far into details here, and will only mention a few of the most conspicuous.

For instance, that of Canon Pettenbeck, kneeling; that of the patrician Eustachius Liegsalz, in full length; and on the sun-dial side, near master Conrad's gravestone, already mentioned, is the stone to the musician Bandinelli, and that of the architect Fischer who built so many churches and monasteries.

Returning to the inside of the church, where I have already called attention to many objects which speak eloquently of strange events, great works, and of people long since passed away, we will look at the beautiful old glass-painting in the windows and especially at those portions which belonged to the first little church of St. Mary, and now in some instances form a part of the large windows painted later, towards the end of the fifteenth century, by Eginhard Trautenwolf.

Furthermore the round escutcheons on the walls.

And the fine old gravestone with it's touching memory of Bishop Tulpekh[1]) of Freising who was present at the laying of the corner-stone of the cathedral, and who afterwards gave up his high position to become pastor of Unser Frauen in Munich.

And the madonna[2]) which he donated.

And the tombstone of Dr. Johannes Neuhauser, near by, who was the first incumbent pastor of the cathedral.

The spiral staircase behind the high altar, near the sacristy deserves a look, for long ago, the lords of Bavaria used to ascend it every Maundy-Thursday, following the Holy Wafer, when it was carried up to the Salvator, or Andreas altar, which was formerly at the top of the staircase.

That altar is remarkable in itself as it is said to have been the high altar in the little church which stood in the middle of the spot now occupied by the Jesuit or St. Michael's church.

The gravestone of the architect of the cathedral has already been mentioned, but I would like to insert

---

1) In the first chapel on the left entering from the big door.
2) Also in the first chapel from the left of the big door.

the inscriptions under his likeness and that of his head carpenter which are on the wall near the organ loft.

The architect's inscription is the same as that on his gravestone.

That of the carpenter, who according to tradition was named Heimeran, is the following;

"This is the true effigy, three hundred years old, of the carpenter of this city, who put his greatest work into this world-renowned basilica, in the ingenious upper storey or roof, for which he used 1400 floats of 15 or 16 trees each. He left a hewn "dram" or beam, as well, which was intended for a certain place. Let no one pass it by. God give him eternal rest."

Anyone may see the aforesaid beam in one of the steeples.

The copy of Michael Angelo's last Judgment[1]) which was formerly on the left of the entrance to the Franciscan church, was painted by the Munich artist Hans Mielich for the tomb of the chancellor Leonard Eck. Our clever historian Lipowsky saved it from the auctioneer's hammer, Ao. 1802, as it was about to be sold for a few marks and end no one knows where.

The tall clock[2]) of Unser Frauen is an example of the ingenuity of mechanics in olden times. Some one has described it thus:

"At the stroke of twelve the Heavenly Father draws his sword, but at the prayers of our Lord Jesus and of Mary, He sheathes it again; the lips and

---

1) Now in Raum 32 of the National Museum, formerly in Unser Frauen.

2) In the first chapel at the left of the big door.

hands of all the figures move as if they were preaching repentance; on the top is a cock which appears before the clock strikes and flaps it's wings and crows, whereupon St. Peter comes out weeping bitterly because he has betrayed Christ, but the Lord approaches him and looks lovingly at him before he is led before Pilate."

Another memorial in Unser Frauen which must not be overlooked, is the tablet[1]) to Pope Pius VI, who on the third of May Ao. 1782, when he was passing through Munich on his way to Vienna, read mass at the altar to the left of the high altar.

The inscription reads:

Pius VI Pontificum max. primus ad hanc urbem invisit Caroli Theodori Ducis Electoris amicus et gratissimus hospes, ipsoque hoc loco sacra peregit III Cal. Maii MDCCLXXXII.

Among other interesting relics is a metal crucifix generally called the black crucifix, in the sacristy. A lieutenant who died about 1730 is said to have worn it on his breast when he was in battle, and to have been saved from death by it several times, the bullets only hurting the feet of the crucifix. When it was silvered over, later, an attempt was made twice to steal it but the thieves did not succeed either time and got away with a bad fright.

Further, the votive-picture[2]) presented by the city of Braunau on the occasion of a great fire.

And then returning to the steeples of Unser Frauen we must not forget two vivid reminders of

---

1) Behind the high altar at the right.
2) In St. Benno's chapel, the fifth on the left from the big door.

the past which ring out from them at certain times, namely, the glorious tones of the great salva bell on high church festivals, and of the smaller one on the festivals of the Holy Virgin.

The ringing of Ave Maria was granted by Pope Bonifaz, at the request of the dukes, Stephan and Friedrich in 1390.

Only two lines are engraved upon the small salva bell.

"In the year MDCXVII after God's birth, I was smelted,

By Master Barthm. Wengle of Munich, inflexible."

There is much more on the large one.

"I am called Susanna and I was made in honor of Jesus, Luke, Mark, Mathew and John. His highness the prince and lord Albrecht, palsgrave of the Rhein and duke of upper and lower Bavaria, was my donor. I was brought from Regensburg. I drive away bad weather and spy out death. Hans Ernst smelted me when the date after God's birth was one thousand four hundred and three and ninety."

The big salva bell weighs 12,500 pounds and the small one 6060.

Now that I have mentioned twenty-eight objects of interest on the outside and inside of the Frauen cathedral, I will leave you to make further discoveries for yourselves and will look about for something else in the city.

My 29th is the archway leading into Lederer strasse from the old Burg. It is said the citizens had to build it for the dukes in those times when the people were beginning to grow rebellious, for which they paid dearly afterwards.

The archway reminds me of a certain court-fool who foresaw what was coming, but his dukes would not believe him and threatened him with imprisonment for his poor opinion of the people of Munich.

Many authors have confused that fool with the wicked burgomaster who was imprisoned in the little Faust Tower, and I got into a serious dispute about it once with a learned professor, who was unusually well-versed in that branch. It ended well, however, because the learned professor admitted, at last, that I was right.

Now, some reminiscences of a dark and dismal hue are coming.

30. The first of these doleful anecdotes concerns the T on a house[1]) in Kaufingerstrasse on the left going from Marienplatz.

That T stands for death (Tod) and the house in question was one of those which died out entirely during the plague of 1634—35. But the particular saying about this one is; an avaricious heir could not control his eagerness to take possession of his property and going into the house too soon after the plague was supposed to have left it, he became it's last victim, and died.

31. The second is an example of cruelty and hate in old times, namely the lower vault of the bakers' house in Gruftstrasse.

A synagogue stood upon the spot formerly and in it, Ao. 1285, a number of Jews were burned alive

---

1) Some relics from that house are to be seen in the Stadt Museum.

at the instigation of the people because there was a
rumor that a Christian child had been murdered by
Jews. A good many years later the building was
turned into a church with small altars in the upper
and lower stories, and because one had to go down
to it by stairs, it was called Gruft (pit) church[1]).

Descriptions and inventories concerning the church
which was still there when I was a boy, were to be
found in the record office of Starnberg up to a few
years ago, when I believe they were removed to the
imperial registry office in Munich.

32. The third is likewise a reminder of trouble
brought about by religious disputes, and this time it
is among Christians themselves, in the Thirty Years
War. The monument I mean, is not in Munich, it is
true, but outside the city at Ramersdorf. Those for
whom it is a memorial belonged to Munich, however,
and the monument was erected in grateful memory
to the members of the clergy and laity portrayed upon
it, who were taken by Gustav Adolf as hostages, in
1630, and who did not return until they had endured
bitter suffering.

33. The fourth is also a memorial of self-sacrificing
patriotism, namely the monument in the Munich
cemetery to the Highland peasants, who fell in the
battle of Sendling, Ao. 1705, fighting for their absent
elector, Max Emanuel, in the war of the Spanish
Succession, and during the Austrian occupation of
Munich.

---

1) It stood back from the corner of Theatiner and Gruftstrasse
— where the back part of the police building is now.

The grave itself with a fine, simple monument of it's own, is, as everyone knows, in Sendling graveyard.

34. Another solemn but less tragic memorial is the Augustine sun-dial[1]) in the courtyard of the district court of Munich. In the last third of the eighteenth century, that sun-dial was looked upon as a means of prophesy, because it had shown the exact time without any sunshine, at which Elector Max III died.

35. The quaint and beautiful little church of St. Johannes in Sendlingerstrasse bears witness to the magnanimity of two brothers named Asam, who were both excellent artists, one in painting, the other in sculpture and stucco-work. The church is a wonderful example of the ornate style of architecture of that period. Later, the two brothers built a house for themselves in Thalkirchen where they spent their old age.

36. The old targets[2]) which hang in the corridors of the shooting-gallery on the hill near Theresien-wiese, are records of many a riflematch and festivities connected therewith, and if one looks at them under-standingly one may read interesting tales.

37. A living memorial is revived every few years, namely the Schäffler (cooper) dance, which is a reminder of a time in the dim past, when the plucky coopers first danced, in order to inspire others with their courage. (Note 1.)

Some of you may think that I have finished the

1) On the left entering the monastery courtyard from Ett-strasse.

2) They are now in the new shooting gallery outside the city near Mitter Sendling.

chapter now, which is a great mistake. But I shall leave those subjects, which are recorded by tablets and monuments and turn to a few which are not generally regarded as important.

38. The broken piece of wood[1]) near the Christoph stone, in the Residenz entrance, has been a bone of contention more than once, but the solution is simple, namely, that the court servants used to put out their torches with it.

An anecdote about the court-fool, Pranger, is connected with this snuffing-out ball.

In the later days of Elector Karl Theodor, a certain foreign nobleman was high in favor and took many liberties upon himself.

One evening when the court servants were putting out their torches, Pranger took his place near the corner and kept shouting "One more!"

The courtiers did not know what he meant, as all the torches had been extinguished, and the foreign nobleman went up to him and said "Don't shout so, Pranger, there is nothing more to be put out!"

"You ought to know", said Pranger. "Out with you!"

Said the nobleman: "You are nothing but a fool."

Answered Pranger: "And you nothing but a light that is nearly spent."

Said the other very angrily: "What do you mean by that?"

Answered Pranger: "Not today, ask me tomorrow.

1) It is no longer there, and seems to have disappeared entirely.

— Complain of me if you like, to His Most Serene Highness!"

And he pushed through the crowd and disappeared.

The nobleman hurried upstairs, and requested an audience, because Pranger had insulted him. He received answer that the Elector had no time: when he went the next morning, the answer was the same — and when he went for the third time in the afternoon, a letter was given him, in which he read that his services were no longer required, for certain reasons — and he realized that his light had really gone out just as Pranger had said the evening before.

39. The stone relief[1]) near Damenstift church with some little dogs and a ball upon it, is probably a memorial of no very important event. There are different opinions about it.

Some say a cannon-ball once flew in that direction and dogs played with it. Others, that dogs and four-footed animals in general, were fed on that spot which accordingly went by the name of the animal's kitchen, "Kuchel" in Bavarian dialect. A long time afterwards, some one wishing for an appropriate ornament for his house remembered vague tales about four-footed animals in which "Kuchel" had become confused with "Kugel" (ball) and the aforesaid relief was the result.

40. There was formerly a warning to all wicked miserly fellows, on a house in Dultgasse on the Anger, in the shape of an angel holding some scales, with a little pure soul in one side and a devil in the other, and the soul weighed most.

---

1) Hackenstraße No. 10.

The origin of the relief was as follows: A hard-hearted old creditor compelled the widow of a debtor to have her house sold at auction by the bankruptcy chair[1]) — a relic of the rigor of justice in those times, near the Fischbrunnen (Note 2) — and then after having driven her away, he moved into the house himself. After that, the widow lived in the utmost poverty but in Christian-like patience, until death came to release her, and with her last breath she prayed for the hard-hearted creditor. The latter made a joke of it all, and continued to show the same severity toward several others.

Once in his purse-pride he said to a poor debtor that he would drive him out of his house, unless he gave him his pretty daughter for a wife and when the debtor prayed him for God's sake to have mercy, he exclaimed, "Don't talk about God to me; what I want is money!" While the words were on his lips, he fell down dead before the door of his house, and they put up the above-mentioned tablet[2]), later, as a warning.

41. The Chamber of Treasures has already been mentioned when I quoted the remarkable description by that worthy syndic and knight of Lazarus, Anthoni Wilhelmus Ertel.

In regard to many interesting and more or less valuable objects in the Treasure Chamber, the Reiche Kapelle, the Royal Library, and the National Museum, I am sorry to be obliged to omit most of them —

---

1) The old Gant Stuhl is said to be in existence still, probably in some storage room.

2) No trace remains now.

for they all speak either of the transientness of power and glory, or of religious austerity and simple piety, or, as in many cases they are merely reminders of some former event; and of these latter much could be written, as I have already done in another book.

To take a few instances only, I will mention the royal crown of Friedrich V of Bohemia, which fell into the hands of our great Elector Max I after the noted battle on the white Mountain near Prague.

Among the costly treasures of the Royal Library, the so-called Cimelian collection, are many objects which bear witness to the religious enthusiasm which was a trait of many of our princes, and to that passion for art which took no thought of expense, like the prayer-book of Emperor Ludwig, or the lovely designs and colors of H. Mielich in the book of psalms, with music by Orlando di Lasso. That world-renowned composer, after many adventures, came to Munich in the last half of the sixteenth century, where he received many honors at court. His church music gives many great pleasure today.

Orlando di Lasso's gravestone[1]) is in the National Museum.

On the outside of the collection's new building[2]) is a peasant's figure with a flag. It is in memory of Balthasar Mayr, the strong smith of Kochel and of those mountain-peasants, who as before mentioned, showed such patriotism in the battle of Sendling at the beginning of the eighteenth century.

---

1) In the entrance hall.
2) Now occupied by the deutsche Museum in Maximilian-strasse.

As I have already said, I cannot go into the particulars of the inexhaustible material for information of past times which the museum furnishes, with it's altars and carved and painted saints and effigies, weapons and armor, household articles, and innumerable other things, and will only speak of a few which bear directly upon my subject, in that legends and tales are connected with them.

A very old statue of the Virgin which was originally in the old Anger church was found a few years ago very much damaged in a woodshed. The good nuns, some time at the beginning of this (19th) century, wanted to have it restored but the money failed them. So it was not put back in it's place but was shoved here and there, suffering much from hard usage, and at last was forgotten altogether. Finally the director of the National Museum, Freiherr von Aretin, found it in it's hiding place, had it repaired so well that no one would notice any damage, and placed it in the collection[1]).

That statue of the Virgin is remarkable enough in itself, because it dates from the ancient times of Duke Otto des Erlauchten who first brought the barefooted monks to St. Jacob's chapel. They stayed in their little monastery for sixty years, until Duke Ludwig der Strenge gave them eight thousand gulden, and commissioned them to build a church and monastery near the castle which he had just begun, namely on the spot where the Royal Opera House now stands. After that change, the little monastery

---

1) No. 6 in Raum 7.

on the Anger was quite deserted and so the rich Sendling people sent to Ulm for Klarissen nuns, and in that manner, on St. Gallus day, Ao. 1284, the convent on the Anger was started.

The stone image, moreover, is a reminder of Emperor Ludwig der Bayer and his first wife Beatrix, and Margarethe his second, all of whom often prayed before it — and especially of a daughter of the two first named, the beautiful princess Agnes, who had an unspeakable longing for a life of holy solitude. She loved to pray in the little church, and could hardly be induced to leave it, until at last it came to light, that her thoughts were far removed from earthly things, and that her one desire was to enter the convent. So after much consideration, the Emperor could no longer say no, and Agnes became a nun, and led a holy life until Ao. 1352. She died in the month of March. Her bones lie in the crypt of Unser Frauen, in the same coffin with those of Barbara, daughter of Duke Albrecht III, who was sent to the convent on the Anger at a tender age, where she died, after hoping in vain to marry a French prince.

She was seventeen years old when she died, Ao. 1472. In the same coffin are the remains of Maria Anna Carolina Josepha Dominika, a sister of Phillip Wilhelm, palsgrave of Neuburg, who took the veil, Ao. 1719, in the presence of Elector Max Emanuel, and his whole court, in the church on the Anger, and in Ao. 1750, departed to God.

The epitaph upon the coffin in which these three princesses lie is; Ossa Clarissarum in Angere D. B.

A relic of the Electress Adelheid of Savoy, wife

of Ferdinand Maria, and foundress of the Theatiner church, is in the Museum, namely her horse hair penance-girdle.

She probably wore it in Holy Week and on those days when the "slaves" or "handmaidens of the Queen of Heaven" as her order was called, had especial services — that is, on all the Virgin festivals.

Adelheid founded the order and was it's lady superior. The garb of the order was a light grey silk robe with a steel girdle, the scapular was dark blue, a white nun's veil hung from the head, and upon the breast was a gold cross on a gold chain.

In this habiliment Adelheid of Savoy was wont to receive the holy sacrament on the days of the Virgin, in Theatiner church with the other sisters of the order, and on Good Friday, they all went in a procession behind the chapter cross to all the graves, and prayed in all the churches of Munich.

She was buried in those garments, like all the sisters of the order, in accordance with the rule.

She was a kind and good sovereign and her heart was full of love for the poor.

The ringing of the bell, three times, and the exposure of the Holy of Holies, before which two Theatine monks prayed when anyone was dying, date from her time.

As much as I should like to chat longer about the museum in question, just so much would I like to talk about the city-armory[1]) on the Anger, wherein there are many curious things, reminding one of princes

---

1) Now the Stadt Museum.

or of notable events, like the sword of Maximilian I. and other weapons. You will hear about a couple of wheels later.

And in the armory near the Hofgarten are a still greater number of curiosities.

In can only make a passing remark here about the giant shoe of Bavaria, which is on the second floor at the side, and which was carried in the great Bavarian Festival procession through the streets of Munich.

There is no question that this largest shoe[1]) in the world will sometime end in the National Museum where it will remind coming generations of the merry festivities of olden times.

And now I would like to tell you about a certain copper gravestone, and a sacristy and then about two buildings of which little now exists in the one case, and nothing at all in the other.

42. The gravestone is that under the organ of the Heiligen Geist church in the Thal, with the figure of a knight upon it.

It represents Duke Ferdinand, brother of Wilhelm V. der Fromme; the same who, A. Do. 1588, renounced his claim to the throne in order to marry beautiful Maria Pettenbeck, and they lived together after that in his house[2]) on Rindermarkt where an alley leads to Rosenthal. Behind in the direction of the latter were the ducal gardens; and at the left

---

1) It is now in the storage room of the Museum.

2) A tablet marks the house, where Duke Ferdinand's palace stood, Rindermarkt 6.

towards the Gate was the church of St. Sebastian
belonging to the royal household. The statue in
question was placed in that church at the death of
the Duke, where it remained until the church was
torn down, then it was brought to Heiligen Geist
church. The bodies of the Duke and his wife, however,
lie in Unser Frauen.

The eight sons and eight daughters besides other
descendants of Ferdinand and the fair Maria Pettenbeck, or Peter Beck's daughter, whose love affair is
told in my "Münchner Stadt Büchlein", received the
title of counts and countesses of Wartenburg, which
lies in lower Bavaria, between Freising and Landshut;
but as a general thing they were simply called the
"Ferdinands" as distinguished from the "Wilhelms"
who were the ruling dukes. The shield of the Warten-
burgs shows the golden Palatine lion on all fours
with a red crown, the shield being checkered in blue
and silver, the crowned helm has a field twice quartered
and bordered with leaves, in the middle of which is
the Palatine lion on its haunches. The house of
Wartenburg did not last very long and died out
completely, Ao. 1736, with an eighteen-year-old count
by name Maximilian Emanuel, who lost his young life
by means of a peachstone in the Academy of Knights
at Ettal.

But to return to the metal statue. It reminds
us of how much more powerful love is than the
magnificence of courts and hope of ruling, and furthermore when one considers the times of Ferdinand and
his part in the wars — especially his attack upon a
certain Gebhard, bishop of Cologne, who wanted to

marry, but still keep his office in the church — we are reminded that catholics were no more of one mind then, than they are now.

So much for the copper statue.

43. In regard to the sacristy, I mean that of the old Residenz chapel, in its relation to our old long-suffering Elector, Carl Albert, or Carl VII., as he was called, as German Emperor.

He came during his last campaign against Austria, Ao. 1744 on the 17th of December, to his capital, Munich, which had just become free again, entering with the Empress and his two youngest princesses, and the whole court, and on December 26th the city of Munich renewed it's oath of fealty to him, a super-fluous act really, because a Bavarian is seldom anything else than faithful to his word.

Be that as it may, the Emperor was there again in the apartements to the right of the court chapel, and although ailing and easily wearied, he was full of hope that in the coming spring, he would get back the upper Palatinate and Danube territory, which were still in Austrian hands.

All at once new clouds began to gather.

On the 15th of January 1745, namely, the Emperor became seriously ill, and although the doctors did their best, the disease conquered and a time of undeniably mortal danger approached.

When the Emperor, himself, became aware of it, someone who ought to know, says that he commanded them to carry him into the sacristy of the court chapel where he could see a little house-altar from his bed.

Then on the morning of the 10th of January, he had his whole family called together and he declared his son, Max Joseph III., to be of age, thereupon he took a loving farewell of them all, and talked awhile with the two dukes of Zweibrücken, then he asked for the last sacrament; at noon they gave the Emperor a tincture of gold, which had such a good effect, that for a few hours, his recovery seemed possible, but that hope did not last long.

Toward seven o'clock, the hour of death approached, and the Emperor left this world, in which his nobly-meant efforts had so often met with bitter disappointment.

Writers of his time, in speaking of him say that his intelligence was great, and that he was full of kindness and affection and bravery, and that he loved entertainments and pomp and glory.

"He had a deep understanding for the affairs of the country, and as to his expenditures, knew how to preserve the balance in the chamber of finance, so that no great want of proportion became visible. He never was the tool of his counsellors, although he gathered good ones around him; but, that he gave more hearing to the French minister, Chevalier de Chavigny than was welcome to that gentleman himself, during his last years — was a most deplorable pity; that was due principally to those cursed times of wars and alliances."

Perhaps you may like to hear something about the Emperor's funeral.

It took place on January 25th at five o'clock in

the evening amidst the tolling of all the bells, and twenty-four knights carried the coffin alternately.

They were preceded by all the different fraternities and orders of Munich, carrying lighted wax candles and praying loudly. Then the musicians and the whole clergy, the court-chaplain and the rector of Unser Frauen, Franz von Bettendorf in pontificials and after them came chaplains and choristers.

Pages with lighted wax candles walked behind the coffin and all the imperial ministers and councellors with lighted candles.

The Theatines who received the coffin at the entrance of their black-draped church, where lights burned at all the altars, accompanied it to the middle, where a hundred candles burned around a black catafalque.

The coffin was placed upon the catafalque and upon nine white cushions they laid the imperial and electoral insignia, as well as that of the golden fleece, and of St. George and other high orders to which the Emperor belonged.

When the requiem had been sung, and the soldiers outside at Schwabing Gate, had fired a salute three times, the coffin was carried by eight gentlemen-in-waiting to the choir, where it was given over to the lord high steward, and formally received into keeping by the pastor of Theatine church, and after the signing of the legal papers, it was carried down into the crypt to the singing of Benedictus Dominus Israel.

Upon the day after the burial, the court-chaplain, Hofreiter, read a funeral sermon which was followed by a mass with music, during which the young Elector Max Joseph III., his mother and sisters, and the whole court, went from altar to altar, making their offerings.

44. Now come the two buildings of which I spoke. There are very few traces left of the first of them, the Neuveste. There are many people who do not know in what order the old castles of Munich were built and at whose instigation: I would gladly explain all that here, had I not already done so in my "Plauderstüblein". But in regard to the Neuveste: It stood upon the open spot, which Allerheiligen church and the back of the Residenz skirt, and we hear of it as early as the end of the fourteenth century; at first it consisted of one small building not far from a stately round tower; later, in the time of Duke Albrecht der Weise it was enlarged.

From then on, that remarkable prince lived in the Neuveste, leaving the old Burg to be occupied by Bavarian or foreign princes visiting here, and by certain high officials, to say nothing of the library which Albrecht placed there. His successors lived in the Neuveste up to the time when it was destroyed by fire. After that, Elector Maximilian I. lived for a few years in the castle which his father Wilhelm V. had built, namely Wilhelm- or Maxburg, and in the first third of the seventeenth century, he commissioned that great master, Peter Candid, to build a new and splendid castle which we now call the Old Residenz as distinguished from the new or restored parts which we call the Residenz.

The old Neuveste castle itself, therefore, is no longer to be seen, but certain buildings at the right and left of the above-mentioned open space, bear evidence to the time when the castle was there, although that at the right has lately suffered changes.

45. The building of which absolutely no traces exist was the Beautiful Tower which was formerly at the end of Kaufingerstrasse not far from the Augustine church.

One sees pictures and descriptions of it in many books, but most people would have forgotten all about it, were it not for the following incident.

At the time of the seven-hundredth anniversary of the city of Munich, when great fêtes and processions took place, a certain worthy doctor and dentist conceived the idea of decorating his house with a plaster-cast of the tower, and asked me for a rhyme in old German to put upon it.

I was naturally very willing, like that schoolmaster and poet who composed the verses for the baker's house in the Thal. So I wrote my lines and gave them to the man, who had them copied on two long rolls and they were fastened up on each side of the miniature tower where they remained all through the festivities.

Afterwards, the little tower stayed on the house, but the scrolls were taken down, and the old German rhymes were cut into a stone tablet with the relief of the tower, over the door.

And what happened then? Nearly opposite the house with the rhymes, is that old Ettal house with the Emperor's fresco, but of course entirely changed now, of which you have already read. A merchant had his shop in that house, and one day, the thought occurred to him that it was a pity there was no reminder of Emperor Ludwig there now.

Thereupon he had a relief of the Emperor made and when it was ready to be put upon the house, he asked for permission from 'the city authorities to do so, but he had to wait long before receiving an answer.

The merchant began to lose patience and thought, "if one's good intentions are not better received, it is all the same to me", and was on the point of giving up the whole thing.

As chance would have it, that same merchant fell into a conversation with the doctor and dentist, and the end of it was, that the latter became the owner of the relief of the Emperor. And no sooner was that the case, than he had it put up on his house[1]) over the little tower, near the rhymes. At the next Corpus Domini procession, there was the whole memorial in plain sight, and no one had a word of blame either for the dentist Meyer or for the merchant Leuze.

And it would be a pretty pass of things if the city officials should forbid our putting up private memorials to our illustrious princes and beautiful buildings of olden times.

In order that anyone who wishes may at his ease, read the rhymes up on the house, I will insert them here.

> "Many hundred years ago
> The city ended here
> It was called the upper Gate

1) No. 20 Kaufingerstrasse.

And a bridge was here as well.
Nearby, the records say,
One saw a field of oats.

Emperor Ludwig was living then,
That noble lord and German hero.
Then the city was enlarged
And they built the Beautiful Tower
The ditch and bridge were seen no more
And the tower was covered with frescoes.

Heralds and trumpeters one saw,
And the Emperor as well.
And all the
Electors at his side
And down below them on the tower
Was a little peasant digging.

And up above the tower, there was
A weatherball most wondrous,
At the golden side good weather
Came, but stormy at the blue.
What was and is, will vanish,
God's love for Bavaria endures."

In Ao. 1807 the tower was torn down. There was much dispute about it at the time, but one side conquered by insisting it was in a dangerous condition. That was surely not so; they only wanted to get rid of beautiful old buildings. I am sure the tower was firmer then, than any new one would be, which all the architects put together, could build now.

46. Opposite the merchant's shop, at No. 12 Kaufingerstrasse, our historian Lorenz von Westenrieder, lived for forty years.

We Bavarians cannot estimate that noble man with his ideal character, too highly, and the influence his works, often written during times of great physical suffering, had upon the state, church and domestic life. So I feel justified in giving a few particulars about him; not about his works, for anyone may read them, but about his parentage, friends, and departure from this life, in short, the questions one asks oneself when standing before his statue[1]).

Well then, on the first of August 1748, Westenrieder first saw the light of this world, in Munich. His father, Christian, was a grain-merchant, and his mother's name was Margreth, and Lorenz went to St. Peter's school.

At about that time Christian died and Lorenz acquired a step-father, one of the best sort, however, who took good care of the boy, and let him go on studying and learning up to Ao. 1771, when he read his first mass, on October 6th, in Unser Frauen.

Westenrieder began his clerical career in a small way, but he rose rapidly and Ao. 1807, he was appointed canonical counsellor, and 1821, a member of the cathedral chapter; that was the same year, in which an agreement was made between King Max Joseph and the papal chair to restore the bishoprics with their chapters, which had been dissolved eighteen years before.

I will mention in passing, that in that year, also, on the first of November, the archbishop of Munich and Freising, Freiherr Anselm von Gebsattel, was ordained bishop, by the papal ambassador, Prince Serra Cassano, in St. Michael's, and on the fifth, held his entry of state into Unser Frauen cathedral.

_____

1) In Promenadeplatz.

But to return to Westenrieder. During his later years, he was one of the oldest members of the Academy of Sciences, which Elector Max III. had founded.

It goes without saying, that Westenrieder was loved and revered by all who knew him, but his chosen friends were; the learned rector of Engelbrechts Münster, Antonius Bucher; the historian, Lorenz Hübner; the Bavarian historians, Roman Zirngibl and Hermann Scholliner; Joseph Orgel, librarian of Ingolstadt; Hueter, priest and school-rector of Straubing; the talented and always merry-tempered Antonius Nagel, rector of Marching, and lastly, his publisher, the well-known J. B. Strobl of Munich.

One day, after Westenrieder was very old, and had left most of his life's work behind him, he was talking with Count Preysing von Moos, who was older still, when the latter remarked; "I am going to the baths of Gastein and shall celebrate my bath jubilee, for this will be no less than my fortieth consecutive summer there."

And Westenrieder answered:

"I cannot say as much as that, but still, I have been going every summer for twenty-four years, and so next year I can celebrate my twenty-fifth jubilee."

Whereupon Preysing replied: "That is not so good as mine, but still, it is something."

But while Westenrieder was looking placidly forward to 1829, Heaven was ordaining it otherwise. For he became ill, and on the 15th of March his soul had passed away.

There was much mourning at that news, and crowds ascended the three flights of stairs to look once more, face to face, upon "noble Westenrieder" to whom the landlord of the house showed hospitality to the very last. For the coffin rested upon a stately catafalque, amid masses of flowers, and many lights, and the room was draped in black, with candelabra of lighted candles on the walls.

On the 18th of March, at four o'clock in the afternoon, the city-chaplain came to accompany the body with lighted torches and sound of trumpets to it's last resting place.

The procession went through Kaufinger, Rosen, and Sendlingerstrasse.

Many members of the Academy of Sciences and University, many high officials, all the city counsellors, the clergy of the three city parishes, the alumni, and a great number of citizens and other people walked in the procession. And so they carried that true-hearted Bavarian to his grave, at the left of the entrance to the arcades in the big cemetery.

Heckenstaller, the dean of the cathedral, gave the benediction, and a beautiful, touching oration.

The landlord of the house had a bust of Westenrieder put up in the room in which he died, and his successor holds it in the same honor; whoever lodges in that room, is expected to see that no harm comes to it.

A few words about the likenesses in existence of Westenrieder.

His friend and admirer, J. B. Strobl, had a steel medallion made by Scheufele. Westenrieder's likeness

12*

is upon one side, and an open book resting upon clouds, with the trumpet of fame, is upon the other.

The inscription is:

Lor. Westenrieder
Natus Monachii. I. Augusti.
MDCCXXXXVIII.
Historiae Boicae Scriptori.
Johann Bapt. Strobl, civis et Biliopola
Monacensis.
Fieri. Curavit. MDCCLXXXVI.

In the last mentioned year, namely, Westenrieder published his "History of Bavaria" in one volume, which was followed, Ao. 1798, by the "Sketch of Bavarian History".

There are three painted portraits of Westenrieder. That by Moriz Kellerhoven is in my possession, and is the best likeness of him; many engravings have been made from it, and are to be seen in some editions of his works.

I often look up at the painting and say "That man is an example of integrity and tireless devotion to our beautiful Bavaria".

47. Now, we will return to olden times and to the court-chapel of the old Residenz, where the likeness of a Carmelite, Dominicus a Jesu Maria, is preserved. He was an ardent supporter of the Emperor and the true faith, and is supposed to have played an important part in the battle of Prague. With the cross of Christ raised high in his hand, he spoke such inspired words to the Duke, later Elector Max I., and to the soldiers, and led them on in such disdain of

death, that no one doubted the victory would be theirs.

In speaking of our great Elector again, it occurs to me that some of my readers may like to know where the best likenesses of him are, aside from the glorious equestrian statue on Wittelsbachplatz, and how he looked at different ages.

The best likeness of him as a child is at the end of the little family-likeness book of his father, Wilhelm V., which book is in the sixteenth-century room in the National Museum; one sees him as a dauntless, steady-eyed youth, in a hall of the old Residenz, at the left, near the Steinzimmer, two flights up from the entrance near the chapel driveway; at the right of the same Steinzimmer, by the way, is a narrow, richly-decorated corridor, with the coats-of-arms of all the Bavarian cities; and his likeness, as an older man hangs in the entrance-hall of the Old Pinakothek on the right.

48. In the church of Herzogspital, is a miracle-working image of the Virgin.

It was made by a certain architect and sculptor named Tobias Bauer, whose likeness is preserved in the sacristy of the same church, and when Elector Max III. was nearing his end, he wished them to bring that image of the Virgin to his bedside. That was accordingly done, and as a contemporary writes, the streets through which they carried it, were filled with people praying upon their knees, for the recovery of their prince, whom they loved like a father, so great was their affection for him.

49. A memorial, speaking of meekness of heart, just as the two last-mentioned tell of trust in and

devotion to the higher powers, is in St. Michael's church opposite the grand monument to Duke Eugen, Viceroy of Italy, and is namely, the plain tombstone of Duke Wilhelm V., the founder of the church; a bronze angel, carrying a holy water vessel stands upon the stone, and the epitaph, expressing resignation to the will of God and longing for forgiveness of each sin of heart, is simply:

Commissa mea pavesco, dum veneris judicare,
Noli me condemnare.

In passing I will mention, that the two bronze lions which are now at the entrance to the old Residenz, were formerly in the choir of St. Michael.

50. Now I wish to call attention to something which no one knows how soon, will be torn down, and that is the oriel tower on the government building[1]) on the market-place. Many high-born personages used to come to Munich, formerly, for the world-renowned Corpus Domini procession; the elder ones used to look on at it from that same tower, while the young and strong walked in it — a matter of several hours, princesses often going with it to show their meekness of spirit. The ruling duke or elector, who walked behind the Holy Wafer, paused at the tower, where a silver goblet was offered him by the mayor, from which he drank. Some consider it was merely a toast of honor, others, that it referred to the blood of Christ.

As I said, there is such imminent danger that the oriel tower will no longer exist, that I did not

1) The government building was taken down in 1866 to make way for the new Rathhaus.

wish to let it pass unmentioned. I shall feel repaid if anyone on his way to market, thinks of it, when he goes by the corner of Dienerstrasse, for it would be a pity were it quite forgotten.

51. Few people know anything about the arched doorway in the house on Max Josephplatz No. 12, and that it was the entrance to the ancient Bittrich or Püttrich convent[1]).

Duke Albrecht IV., or der Weise, as everyone knows, married Kunigunde, the beautiful daughter of Emperor Friedrich III., without the latter's knowledge or consent, and thereby much quarrelling arose, but at last the Emperor became reconciled, and the ducal pair lived together in peace after that.

Albrecht died A. Dom. 1508.

Kunigunde, bowed down by grief, was present at the funeral services for her beloved husband, and then she drove directly to the door of the Bittrich convent, and ringing the bell, she entered, never to come out again, except on one or two occasions which duty made imperative.

So, for me, that arched doorway is a recorder of noble sorrow and anguish; and although I do not doubt that many wives moan their husbands as deeply to-day, still I do not wish that touching example to pass unobserved.

52. In connection with the Corpus Domini procession, which I have mentioned several times, I am reminded of the standards of the different fraternities,

---

1) The convent extended back to Theatinerstrasse. Inscriptions on the house on the corner of Theatiner and Perusastrasse refer to it.

of which there were many in Munich, and of their relation to the church. There were the Congregation of Apprentices, of Gentlemen Citizens, of St. Isidor, of a Peasant, of St. Nothburga, of a Servant Maid, the Angel Fraternity, that of the Seven Sorrows of the Virgin, that of St. Maurizius, of Mary Magdalena, the High Fraternity of St. Michael, of St. Laurence, the Saver of Souls, the Latin Congregation, the Corpus Christi Fraternity, that of St. John Nepomuck, the Altötting Madonna Fraternity and that of St. George Martyr [1]).

How certain of these fraternities influenced art, creating master-pieces which have gone down to posterity, can be seen in one example, that of the Fraternity of Gentlemen Citizens, who, in Ao. 1584 according to the bull of attest by Pope Gregor XIII, combined with the Latin Congregation, appearing in Ao. 1610 as a new and especial League of St. Mary.

Ao. 1710, the fraternity bought with the help of the city, three houses in Neuhauserstrasse, one of which belonged to Freiherr von Lerchenfeld, and two to lawyer Biedermann, and these they rebuilt into the "Bürgersaal"; then they sent for the celebrated Tyrolese painter, Knoller, and commissioned him to paint the Ascension of the Virgin, on the ceiling of the church, a picture which is much admired to-day. The landscape painter, Beich, was commissioned to paint the Bavarian crusades for the same church, and it is said that he did it for such a small price, that his own

---

1) The banner of the fraternity of St. George, dating 1562 is in Raum 78 of the National Museum.

expenses could hardly have been covered. And his pictures may, therefore, be looked upon as an offering to the Virgin.

So much for the naïvely, and in many cases beautifully, painted standards, and for the masterly, big church paintings.

53. This or that picture or inscription on some particular house has already been mentioned. There is no need of describing the fine biblical scenes[1]) on certain houses in Kaufingerstrasse as they speak for themselves.

But there are two frescoes[1]) on the right, just as one enters the Thal from the Rath Tower, which represent former costumes and trades. One was donated by the guild it depicts, and one by someone who had been made a burger. The first fresco coming from the Rathhaus is the more interesting, because the old castle of Unter Wittelsbach is seen in the background of the landscape.

As my subject is Old München, I cannot say very much about the frescoes upon the newly restored Rath Tower, but will allow myself the remark that we, as well as coming generations, should be thankful that the city had the money as well as the wisdom and foresight to have it done.

Beside those views of old Munich in the small Rathhaus and in the Pinakothek, there are some remarkable and very ancient frescoes[2]) in the "Alten

---

1) The frescoes no longer exist, but there are pictures of those which were in the Thal, in the Stadt Museum.
2) In Saal 14 of the National Museum.

Hof" or old Ludwig's Burg which were discovered some twelve years, or so, ago. They are called the Fürsten frescoes and are only a part of a whole series of figures of princes with devices, which decorated the courtyard formerly. The wooden post[1]) near by dates from the old Anger church.

54. I promised sometime ago to tell about a couple of wheels in the old armory on the Anger. The tale is as follows:

Ao. 1709, some men were sitting together in St. Jacob, a suburb of Augsburg and one of them had just told about a wheelwright, who seventeen years before, had made a wheel and driven it to Dachau, all on the same day.

The tale was strongly doubted, but a wheelwright, Johannes Guttmann of Lechhausen insisted that he, himself, had been present and that he was ready to do the same thing from Lechhausen to Munich[2]).

A hatter, named Christian Ulber, did not believe he could do it, and offered a bet of thirty gulden, which the other man accepted and the trial was fixed for the twentieth of June.

A few days later, the hatter regretted the bet, but the wheelwright would not let him off, and thereupon the hatter fell into a rage and said such bad things of him, that the wheelwright complained of him to the burgomaster, who decided the matter in favor of the wheelwright. The hatter then offered a compromise of ten florins, and the burgomaster advised

---

1) In Saal 14 of the National Museum.
2) A distance of about thirty miles.

making an end to the affair. Then the wheelwright betook himself to a lawyer, Simon Peter, who said "he must not let them hoodwink him; Weber had made the bet, and if the burgomaster did not think he was in the right, why had he decided in his favor first?"

So Guttmann took courage and waited for the twentieth of June, when he rose very early, and in sight of a crowd of people, among whom were two wheelwrights named Franz Schmucker and Andreas Bloss, who were there as judges of his work, and who handed him his tools, there, in his doorway in full sight of them all, he made the back wheel to a cart. At seven o'clock, it was finished and he went to mass and a benediction was pronounced over him and his wheel. Then Guttmann started on his journey, first drinking a bumper at Hans Jacob Weber's inn, and began rolling his wheel, four Augsburg men, Seehofer, Greimbod, Kuttner and Rechelhammer, riding along beside him. They stopped at Huber's brewery in Friedberg, and the wheel adventure attracted a crowd of people; the shop-keeper, Veit Hörman, being so infatuated, that he ran along, *per pedes apostolorum*, beside the wheel when it started again.

He probably took something to sustain himself on the way, for Guttmann and the four riders stopped eight times, at different signs of inns. In spite of so much tippling, wheelwright Guttmann reached Munich long before the gates were closed.

The news had gone before him and a crowd was assembled to escort him to the royal brewery, the present great public-house at the left, coming in from Neuhauser gate, where the wheelwrights of Munich, headed by the masters Marr Holzmüller and Phillipp Meister, received him, and old Clemens Albrecht offered him a big pewter mug decorated with ribbons, with their congratulations and hearty welcome.

Then they all went up to the dining-room where there was a banquet; the next day Guttmann gave the counsellor a detailed account of the whole affair, and the day after that, he was asked to roll his wheel to the Residenz where the imperial minister of the interior, Count Löwenstein Wertheim, looked at it, talked with the wheelwright, and gave him a present as the counsellor had done, after having written out a testimony for him of his due arrival. Guttmann stayed two days longer in Munich during which time he was well treated by the guild, who gave him another testimonial, and bought his wheel, which they had gilded and hung up in the dining-room, and then he returned to Lechhausen crowned with glory.

So far so good, but after that, a lawsuit about the bet of thirty gulden began, which lasted ten years and was the cause of "much annoyance and great expense."

It went so far that Guttmann suffered assault and battery, of which he bore a sign for the rest of his life, in a "crooked leg, by reason of which, however, an imperial ban was issued upon his enemy Ulber, the hatter."

Sometime later Guttmann was seized again with the wish to drive a wheel to Munich, which he carried out, in spite of his crooked leg, and that last wheel was hung up with the first one[1] in the armory.

---

1) In Saal 79 of the National Museum.

55. I have already had a good deal to say about churches and their religious or admonitory meaning for us, and now I will mention one, which was connected with political affairs, namely, the church of Dreifaltigkeit (Trinity), not far from Maximilianplatz. On the outside of the church is an inscription from the three "status boici" and inside are two memorial tablets at the left and right of the organ. It is a votive-church, owing it's existence to a prayer to heaven to avert the danger of war which was threatening at the beginning of the eighteenth century. Although a good deal of misfortune happened in the first decade of 1700, still, it might have been much worse. At any rate, those who had made the vow, felt called upon to keep their word, and the church was built as it now stands, comely on the outside and full of religious sentiment, inside.

Not far from that church, going towards Maximilian-platz, and diagonally opposite Wilhelm- or Maxburg, stood the electoral ball-game house.

If it stood there still, it would be looked upon as a curious old reminder of the way people used to amuse themselves.

But there was something else connected with it. One day, namely, in 1632, the Swedish king, Gustave Adolphus was playing ball there in the big hall with his generals and other high lords who had entered Munich with him, and the king showed great dexterity in the game.

Friedrich of the Palatinate, or the Winter king, as he was called, whose crown Elector Maximilian gained possession of, as you remember, was looking on, and he is said to have called out, half maliciously, "That was Prague — this is Munich. His good luck was as fickle as a shuttlecock".

And Gustavus is said to have answered, "So it is still, Fritz! God help us not to bat our luck away and get bad luck batted back at us!"

Those words turned out to be true, for not long after that, the battle took place, in which Gustave Adolphus fell.

56. Now, I want to call attention to the gravestone of rector Ersinger under the organ on the left, at St. Peter's, for it is a fine example of art in those old days. Ersinger was, moreover, one of the few whom Duke Albrecht IV. or der Weise, ever asked for advice, and whose counsel in important affairs he often followed.

That Duke who is important in Bavarian history, for establishing the primogenitur, if for no other reason, was buried in Unser Frauen cathedral, as you already know. Possibly some of you may like to hear about the grand funeral services for him, especially as I have already told about his Duchess Kunigunde, and her drive to the Bittrich convent, after the requiem for her husband had been sung.

A full description is given by a certain old-time author, under the title of "The memorial and funeral procession in high honor of Duke Albrecht IV. in Bavaria Ao. D. in the ninth year" (1509).

The following named were "bidden" to the funeral.

Emperor Max I., friend and brother-in-law of the deceased, two electors, a number of dukes and landgraves and margraves, counts, barons and knights;

further, the Archbishop of Salzburg, provincial bishops, prelates, priests and abbots, as well as the chaplains of Salzburg, Eichstett, Augsburg, Freising and Passau, likewise the counsellors of different cities, far and wide.

A great many of them came in person on the Sunday before St. Sebastian, Ao. 1509, and others were represented by one or more persons, as for instance, Emperor Maximilian, who sent the Dean of the cathedral of Augsburg, and the knight, Adam von Freunds- or Fronsberg. In all, there were a great many more than two hundred princely, clerical and secular lords, to say nothing of their followings. Margrave Friedrich von Brandenburg came with 180 horsemen, for instance, and the Archbishop of Salzburg with the same number; Duke Ulrich of Würtemberg had a suite of 380, the Bishops of Eichstett, Augsburg, Freising and Passau 80, 70, 55 and 50 respectively; and in addition to all those, eighty important clerical and secular gentlemen came "unbidden".

In the meantime Unser Frauen had been draped with "good, black, woolen cloth" and decorated with white crosses and Bavarian coats-of-arms. The bier "hung about with near 40 ells of good, black velvet" whereon was a triple cross with golden flowers, was placed where Emperor Ludwig's memorial stone is now; the "Hochgrab" up in the choir was draped with black and when the ceremonies were about to begin, "over six hundred pounds of wax candles" were lighted, to say nothing of the many hundreds of wax candles which the mourners carried.

The procession into the church began, two by two, with "fifty houses of poor people in long black garments and mourning hoods, each carrying a long candle weighing a pound, with the Bavarian coat-of-arms upon it".

Then came counts, knights, and gentlemen and ladies-in-waiting, who were followed by the Duchess Kunigunde, led by Count von Ortenburg and Hans von Pfeffenhausen; and her two daughters Sabilla and Sabina were accompanied by Johannes von Loitern and Johannes von Aichberg, lord of Hals, and by Wolf von Frauenberg, lord of Haag, and Hieronimus von Stauf auf Ernfels.

They were followed by a long line of counts, barons and knights.

"Then came the herald in mourning garment, and hood, with a long point, his coat-of-mail hanging on his arm, and his staff pointing to earth, in sign that his whilom prince and mighty lord was dead."

After him princes and ambassadors came — a long and imposing array.

They divided upon the two sides of the church. Duchess Kunigunde remained in the centre with her ladies and maids-of-honor, and together with the other ladies who had come from all parts of the country, kneeled upon her chair; behind them were "sixty women and maids from old families of Munich and near them forty nuns. Abbots and priests from the provinces stood in the choir; and next the bier was the herald in his mourning garment".

The service began and "the first office was chanted by Herr Philipp, Palsgrave of the Rhein, Duke in

Bavaria, Bishop of Freising, and his assistants were Count Jörg von Ortenburg, for the Evangelist, and Herr Degenhard von Weichs, for the Epistle".

In the offertory procession, the order was thus. First the herald offered a golden ducat which Duke Albrecht, Ao. 1500, had had coined; he was followed by two friars with burning candles.

Two friars also accompanied those who followed, namely, the knights, Sigmund von Rorbach, and Wendl von Haunburg and after them came Count Christoph von Ortenburg carrying the banner, then Johannes von Degenberg with the sword, Hieronimus von Stauf with the shield, and the high-steward Gregor von Eglofstein and Wolfgang von Frauenberg of Haag, who carried the helm.

Then "six horses, covered down to the ground with black woolen cloth and each with three lighted candles above his forehead, and a shield with the coat-of-arms of Bavaria, hanging on each side, were led around the sacred altar.

The first horse was led by Count Franz von Pasing and Count Wolf von Montfurt. The second by Count von Urych and a young Herr von Lichtenstein. The third by Herr Dätzko, called Würfel, a Bohemian, and Herr Christoph von Laiming, knight. The fourth, Herr Hanns von Closen, knight, and Herr Bernard von Seiboltstorf, knight. The fifth, Herr Wilhelm von Paulstorf, knight, and Herr Wolf von Weichs. The sixth, Herr Peter von Altenhausen and Herr Kaspar Winger, knight."

After them came four noblemen and then the Emperor's envoy, the dukes Wolfgang, brother of Albrecht, and Wilhelm, his eldest son, and a long line of dukes, land-and margraves, abbots, royal and municipal counsellors; among the latter, was that fine Willibald Pirkheimer, counsellor of Nürnberg and particular friend of the great master Albrecht Dürer.

Then the envoys of eight cities of the land came, then many other envoys, counts, knights and noblemen, then the prelates in pontificials, priests, deans and the chaplain of Unser Frauen; then six knights of Bavaria, and then the knight Hieronimus von Seiboltsdorf carrying a large, lighted, wax candle, with one hundred Rheinish gulden stuck into it, and finally, after all these, Duchess Kunigunde went to make her offering, followed by all the maids and women.

I have given a detailed account of the proceedings, so that you may see how the funeral of a prince was carried out in those days, and I will only add that during the services an Augustine father read the sermon and spoke at length of the life and services of Albrecht der Weise, and mentioned many other princes of Bavaria and Habsburg, who had departed this life, commending them to the prayers of Christians; and, after the services were at last ended, Duchess Kunigunde drove away to the Bittrich convent.

The princes, princesses and all the nobles, clerical and secular, returned to the Neuveste, in the same order in which they had come, the young women and serving-maids to the old Burg or to their inns.

I was about to conclude here, when it occurred to me that there is another matter connected with that great funeral ceremony, which might interest some of my readers; namely, the bill-of-fare at the dinner of state, served to the princes, royal envoys, and counsellors in the Neuveste, at four different tables; the others were served from the court kitchen at their different inns. It took place after the morning repast, and after the funeral, at one o'clock after noon, and the seven ages of the world were represented in it.

The aforesaid bill-of-fare was as follows.

First.

"The first age of the world, namely, Adam and Eve in the garden, and between them a green tree, around it, the serpent, with an apple in it's fangs which it held out to Eve and mushrooms and toad-stools made of sugar and almonds.

Second.

A boar's head stewed and then browned on a spit.

Third.

Stewed meat with capon, and chicken and meat in a gravy.

Fourth.

An image of the second age, namely Noah's Ark with wafers baked of sugar.

Fifth.

Hot dishes of fish like salmon-trout, umber and other good varieties.

Sixth.

A sauerkraut and what goes with it.

Seventh.

The third age, namely the figure of Abraham about to offer up his son, and therewith a tower of sugar and almonds.

13 *

Eighth.

A high transparent jelly with fish in it.

Ninth.

Fresh and salted venison with peppers.

Tenth.

The fourth age, namely the little king David standing against Goliath, the giant, with his sling in his hand and sweet crumpets of sugar and almonds.

Eleventh.

A vegetable.

Twelfth.

A stewed or pickled sturgeon.

Thirteenth.

The fifth age, namely the Tower of Babel, standing with some other buildings in a vegetable.

Fourteenth.

A pie with stewed birds in it.

Fifteenth.

A roast of venison with cold chicken in vinegar.

Sixteenth.

The sixth age, namely the birth of Christ. Mary and the child and Joseph and the asses, oxen and manger made of white almond paste.

Seventeenth.

A pie of pears and other vegetables.

Eighteenth.

Stewed birds.

Nineteenth.

The seventh and last age, namely the last judgment, with the Saviour sitting under a rainbow. The

Virgin, as suppliant, on his right, and St. John kneeling at his left, and marzipan of sugar and almonds.

Twentieth.
Carp and waller fish.

Twenty-first.
Roast pheasant, grouse, partridge, birds and other
good game.

Twenty-second.
The gravestone of our gracious lord, Duke Albrecht of blessed memory, with all the flags and banners
of the land and kingdom, just as it stood in Unser
Frauen. Upon the stone, a man in full armor lay,
holding a banner in his right hand and a naked sword
in his left, and two shields were at his feet, one
painted with Bavarian (coat-of-arms), the other with
the eastern countries. Thereby filled wafers."

That was the dinner of ceremony on the funeral
day. There had been one, the day before, and there
was another, the day after, at which it is explicitly
stated, "a pastry in the form of tiles of a stove, was
served, out of which living birds flew." A few of
the dishes served at other times to the guests were
"A galley with tall masts. Our Lady of the Sun,
under a tabernacle upon four pillars. A pastry with
doors inside of which was a pig, and outside a stag
with golden horns. A pelican plucking at it's own
breast from which blood flowed into the nest where
it's young lay. A fountain out of which Rainfal wine
rose, falling again into a trough.

A brown hedgehog in a white vegetable.

Samson sitting on the lion and forcing it's jaws open.

The beheading of St. John. And castles, and the Last Supper, a fine peacock, and a merry chase, all modelled in almond paste."

Lastly, it is recorded that all the princes and ambassadors with their suites, and all the others who came for the funeral, were entertained in all the inns free of cost, whereby it is remarked: "The kitchens and cellars of our gracious lord, produced food for 2500 people daily, and eighteen hundred and sixty horses were fed."

So much for the funeral of Duke Albrecht IV.

57. To touch upon several subjects, now, all of which give material for reflection, I will mention, first, the outside staircase of the Rathhaus[1]), with the window above it; criminels, condemned to death, stood upon the first step of that staircase, while the sentence was read out from the window, and a staff broken over them.

Further; the large audience-room of the Rathhaus, in which several important diets took place, as well as royal weddings, patrician balls, and other events, like the councils of the burghers in times of trouble, about all of which one could tell a long tale. And the small audience-room with the pictures upon it's walls of old and new Munich, recalling those times when we were less politic than now.

Furthermore; not far from the city on the old

---

1) The modern relief on house no. 2 in the Thal shows the staircase on the old Rathhaus.

Augsburg highway, at the left, in a small yard, is the oldest castle boundary stone, and directly opposite, in the so-called Wiesenfeld is a column commemorating that the Isar once flowed there.

Further; in a house on Sendlingerstrasse, is a bullet which flew over from the Gasteig, where the Austrians were stationed, while General Moreau's men were on this side; near the house with the bullet, is one with arches, which dates from the time of Emperor Ludwig.

But to turn to a spot of cheerful memory, which in it's former, romantic chiaroscuro, was probably the cause of many a visit to the "fool's chamber" or ride upon the "punishment donkey" by those who had tarried there too long, and drained too many bumpers. As a general thing, though, the men who frequented it most, were those to whom the noise in the Bürger beerhouse opposite, was annoying, or others of a thoughtful, or melancholy turn of mind, who loved to sit there musing over the sorrows of this world, thereby emptying one bumper of "brown" after another. The place I mean is no other than the beerhouse "zum ewigen Licht" [1]) where the celebrated Herr Petrus Nöckerlein of Vienna often sat, whose life, so full of amusing adventures on one side, and of grave events on the other, I published sometime ago — the same Herr Nöckerlein whom that wild-looking attorney, Bartholomäus Russheimer, persecuted so sharply. That was Ao. 1517, at the time religious strife had begun in Germany, and two beautiful girls were living in

1) Where Peterhof Hotel is now.

Munich, who captured all hearts, namely Elizabeth
Ligsalz and Antonia Bart, between whom Nöckerlein
vacillated so long, that at last he did not get either.

58. Speaking of the attorney, Bartholomäus Ruß-
heimer, reminds me of a certain house in Weinstrasse
opposite the dragon corner, not because the aforesaid
Herr Russheimer, with his big, turned-up moustache,
went there to have a tooth which ached horribly,
removed by the dentist Schneeberger, but did not do
it after all, because the pain ceased every time he
took hold of the door-knob; but because a certain
doctor, Antonius Herbarius, in German, Graser, lived
there later, and whose experience is a warning to
doctors for all time to examine their patients, before
saying what the matter is.

This Herr Doctor Herbarius lived in the little
house just opposite the dragon corner, and it was
said that before he came to Munich, he had lived in
Mayence, and that although he applied leeches, and
plasters to his patients, his favorite remedy was a
certain sizzling, golden-yellow alternating to rose-
colored tincture, which sometimes cured people, who
overcame their repugnance enough to take it, but
more often did not. In the latter case, Herbarius
always insisted they had taken too much or too little,
otherwise they would surely not have died.

Be that as it may, he was celebrated, and there
must have been some reason for it; he left no stone
unturned in supporting and increasing that fame,
however.

For that reason, he ordered people to come as
soon as they saw anyone had gone to him, and

talk in the most confidential way about maladies of the body, poor stomachs, heart-flutterings, sharp pains, and anything they could think of, always remembering to say that no other doctor of Mayence had been able to cure them, in which he always agreed emphatically; or they pretended he had already cured them, although he had never laid eyes upon them, and when it came to the question of his fee, they paid it with the greatest show of joy, but always with Dr. Herbarius' own money which he had given or sent them for the purpose.

Now, all that was not exactly honest looked at from one point of view. But he had a great many enemies, who were always trying to slander him, so possibly it was only a necessary precaution to add as much to his good name, as they were taking away from it, and saying as bad a word for them, as they were saying for him. Seen from that side, it was only an example in equations. We must try to be lenient as well as just, especially to the dead.

But there is no doubt that Herbarius erred deeply in what I am about to relate, and I shall tell it all the more plainly now that I have given him the benefit of the doubt in some of his proceedings.

Well then, while Herbarius was so busy taking care of his fame, and was giving the other doctors a great deal of bother by his ever-increasing reputation and by the noise he made over their tiniest mistakes, he heard one day that the world-renowned doctor Theophrastus Paracelsus was about to come to Mayence.

When Herbarius heard that, he did not like it at all, and he sent at once for people, who in the presence of real patients, said they had consulted Para-celsus in this or that foreign place, but all to no good; whereupon, Herbarius deplored the fact that people let themselves be deceived by such a travelling quack, in spite of the harm they saw he was doing, and the innumerable people he was sending to the grave. That was stratagem! Next, he sent his apprentice, who was in good practice in such duties, around to all the public squares and taverns of the town, to prejudice the people against the man who had the impudence to think of coming to Mayence, possibly to dim the light of his master's fame.

He did his work so well and made the people so suspicious of Paracelsus, by telling of his own master's wonderful cures in contrast to the miserable failures of the other, that in the course of a few days, he had them well in hand, and Dr. Herbarius had little to fear in case Paracelsus should really arrive.

So Herbarius was quite easy in his mind.

His greatest triumph came, however, with the news that Paracelsus had taken another route "because he had other things to do, and had heard moreover, that a feeling against him existed in Mayence, because he had made a mistake in one or two cases. That could happen to the cleverest, and probably had already happened not a few times to Herbarius: it was no very important matter anyway. But all the gossip had robbed him of his desire to see Mayence and he was going straight to Cologne where he was perfectly sure there was no one worthy to tie the latchet of his shoe."

Day by day passed as usual, bringing many

strangers to Mayence, and among them, a certain gentleman in the green chaise from Frankfort.

He descended with difficulty at the inn of the Three Kings, complained somewhat, did not leave his chamber, and at last took to his bed; he told the landlord about his illness and mentioned Theophrastus Paracelsus. "Let everyone beware of him! He, himself, was a warning! He had used an entirely wrong cure for him in his illness, so that on the third day he was so ill, he hardly lived through the night. And he felt the same attack coming on again. So if they could bring a doctor, he would be glad, and if possible, he would like to see Doctor Herbarius of whose cleverness he had heard so much, that he believed if he could not cure him, nobody could, and he would soon be a dead man."

Now Herbarius liked nothing better than performing a miracle, especially when Paracelsus could be harmed by it, so he took out his golden-yellow and pink tincture, at once, as well as his blood-letting instruments and set out for the inn preceded by the apprentice, Christian, carrying leeches, bleeders and plasters, letting a word fall now and then to the people he passed, such as, "That is just like Paracelsus, he spoils the soup and we must make it good! Well, we will do our best, but if he dies, it is not our fault!"

When Herbarius had reached the bedside of the sick man, and saw how black in the face he was, and how he was shaking under the bed-clothes, and how his mouth was twitching, he said to those who had come in with him, "You see for yourselves, what a state the man is in! In all my experience, I never saw anyone so black in the face, and that shaking and twitching are no good signs, either!" Then he turned to the patient and said, "So that is what Theophrastus Paracelsus has done for you! If it is not "dolos" it is at least "kulpose"! that cursed globe-trotter and quack! the murderer! May the devil go off with him to the infernal regions!"

"Yes" sighed the man, "that would be a good thing, and ought to have happened long ago. You ought to be careful, though, if he comes to Mayence, as I heard he is thinking of doing, because he hates you."

"Pah! He won't come," said Herbarius, "he would find it too hot for himself here". "That is fortunate for the people" said the sick man, "because he is an impudent fellow, and if he only gets his money, he does not care how many he sends into the next world. Oh! I feel horribly! Chills are running all over me, and how my face twitches! It is beyond human endurance!"

"So it seems", said Herbarius "but we hope to cure you, only you must have patience. You can be partly cured of the disease itself, but I am not so sure about that black color you have."

"Oh!" said the sick man, "I will be patient enough, if I only come out of it with my life, so that I can take revenge on that Paracelsus! Only think! He gave me medicine for my kidneys and spleen, and for the life of me, I don't believe anything was the matter with them! What do you think?"

"It is ridiculous", said Herbarius, "Kidneys! Spleen! A thousand times more likely it is your liver and spine, may be heart-trouble too, with congestions now and there. Have you ever had congestions?"

"Of course", said the man, "I cannot count how often or how many."

"Just so, and those congestions themselves can prove whether they are "congestiones falsae" which according to my latest theory arise from stomach and head nerves rather than from the blood, a difficult matter to explain to you, as you are not a *medicus*, but that is how it is, and now you know it! Your present illness, however, has nothing to do with all the troubles you may have had formerly."

"Tell me at least, what the name of my present illness is", insisted the man.

"If I only could!" answered Herbarius, "I have certainly seen more illnesses than all the other *medici* put together, especially in Turkish and Hungarian countries, and even in Persia. Sometimes they were so ghastly to look at that I nearly lost my sight, my apprentice, Christian, is witness of it, but I never saw anything to compare with you."

"That is awful", said the sick man, "Oh dear! Oh dear!"

"Yes, you are right", said Herbarius, "but that is of no moment. When I say I do not know what your malady is, I do not mean I shall never know. It is like this: I shall begin the cure with that black color, for I saw at the first glance, that poison caused it, which, however, has nothing to do with the original disease, which had it's source in your own *corpus*, but with the "superfluum venenosum", with which the medicines of that cursed Paracelsus have filled you, and consequently, the first disease is aggravated and is rising with the other to the surface."

"That sounds plausible"; said the other.

"So you see it too", said Herbarius. Now if I get the poison, as such, to transpiring, and apply plasters, cupping and leeching, all at the same time, so that the poison which has appeared on the surface will be drawn out by force, and above all, bleed 12 ounces, whereby your body will be relieved of a good deal of bad blood, and that which is left will be made over into better stuff by means of these two tinctures, you will begin to feel some results."

"No doubt", said the patient.

"So you agree once more", said Herbarius. "And if you really get well, there will be no doubt that the malady was specific poison disease which I will give a name to at once by which all other doctors will have to call it, "morbus pene mortiferus venenosus specialis maximus." You may as well have a little idea of the authority I exercise; every learned word I utter, and every name I give, becomes celebrated far and wide."

"Yes you are world-renowned" murmured the sick man, "otherwise I should not have wanted you so badly."

"And I shall not disappoint you" said Herbarius "Your case is a desperately bad one, but that has it's good side. In what way? Because if an art like mine, cannot help you, it is much better to be dead than alive; but if I succeed, as I hope to do in getting you out of it, your joy and my own will be all the greater."

"Yes, you are right in both cases", sighed the other, "better dead than alive like this! Begin at once and do what you like with me. Only I have one question first; as I am so desperately ill, why is my pulse so steady? I have just been feeling it again, and I tell you, it is going like anyone's. Just feel it yourself."

"May be", said Dr. Herbarius, "but it surprises me so little, that I do not consider it necessary to feel it; the only thing I am interested in at present is that disease which Paracelsus' poisons have caused, and your pulse has nothing to do with that. Besides, you are tall and strongly built and your steady pulse comes from your good constitution, and only proves, at most, that Paracelsus' poisons were cold poisons."

"Yes, that is so", agreed the other "everything he gave me was cold."

"Now, did I not tell you so! If they had been hot poisons your whole artery system would be so inflamed, you could hear your pulse beat."

"What deep knowledge and how few words!" came from the bed. "Begin now! But one word first. You hope to cure me of everything, if it is a possible thing, and if you succeed what will your price be? Demand what is due you, for I am not a poor man".

"Taking your awful condition into consideration", said Herbarius, "the obscurity of the present malady, and the still greater obscurity of the malady I will cure after the first one is out of the way, and considering the possible danger to my prestige, and the value of the gold and precious stones in the tinctures,

I cannot with the best will, make my price less than ten gold gulden. And thereby I am acting with the greatest consideration, in order to spite Theophrastus Pararcelsus, who brought this frightful disease upon you. Let that fellow come here just once, and I will show him a face that will make him take to his heels! I will talk to him till he sees sparks!"

"Oh! If I could only be there to hear it!" said the man in bed. "What would you say to him for instance?"

"I can tell you very easily" and Herbarius doubled up his fist and scowled ferociously. "I would howl at him: You pseudo-celebrated, shamming fellow! You cursed poisoner, you! How dared you, in addition to your other evil practices, poison an honest man through and through, to such a degree, that he nearly died before my eyes!

Ha! You knave! I cured him though! Even if I had not given him any medicaments but had only stayed near him letting him smell of my remedies, even if I had only left them somewhere near him, they very likely would have cured him, they are such strong antidotes! You don't believe it, you scoundrel! But it is so nevertheless!"

"Of course it is" called out the man in bed, "whether he wants to or not! There are your tinctures over there, and here am I, completely cured, all of a sudden!"

Thereupon he sprang out of bed in his deerskin trowsers and slipping into a fur-bordered dressing-gown, he took a sponge from the table, which he passed over his face wiping away all the blacking, and which he then flung at Herbarius shouting, "Now you know whom you have before you! I am Theophrastus Paracelsus whom you have been slandering and defaming, you and your apprentice. Nothing was the matter with me, and that is an end of your "morbus pene mortiferus venenosus specialis maxima!" I have brought your *ignorantia maxima* to light, so get away and begone!"

Thereupon Herbarius and his apprentice made short work of going, and before two days had passed, they had left Mayence, for rumors of what had happened got about, and there was so much talk, that any confidence in him was at an end for ever, and all attempts of the apprentice, Christian, to restore it were fruitless.

Paracelsus himself stayed only a day longer, for he had received a call somewhere else, where he covered himself with much glory, and probably saw to it that the story about Herbarius became known in the whole region.

But as is often the case, time and distance effaced the defeat of Herbarius more and more, the further he travelled. And since Munich is a long way off from Mayence, he settled here at last, which was a very wise thing to do. People in Munich had heard vaguely about Paracelsus, and the lesson he taught another doctor, but they did not know that the latter's name was Herbarius, and the whole rumor was of short duration. So when he settled in Weinstrasse, no one had an idea that he was the one whom Paracelsus had made such a fool of, and the whole story never became known here.

With one exception, when a merchant of Mayence came here and the conversation turned upon Herbarius, in a certain patrician's house.

When the Mayence man heard the name Herbarius, he asked if it was the same who had been in the affair with Paracelsus, and he told all about it, whereupon they said it must have been another Herbarius.

But the merchant was not convinced and when he heard about his manner of treating, he offered to prove it was the same Herbarius, by pretending he was ill, and letting them send for the doctor. He knew that he would recognize him at once if it was the same man.

But Herbarius got wind of it, and when they sent for him, he and his apprentice had gone to Dachau, where he said he had a case.

Before he came back, the merchant was obliged to return home, and as he went out of one gate Herbarius came in at another.

That is the story of Herbarius, and the reason that that house in Weinstrasse is a memorial of the science of medicine in the sixteenth century.

But as regards his practice in Munich, they said his cures were not always as unfortunate as they might have been, although as a general thing, he killed oftener than he cured.

There is an account too, of how he married a very charming but penniless girl in his old age, with whom he lived very happily, and she was not ill for a long time. But when she did fall ill once, he called in another doctor. At the latter's question why he did not cure her himself he answered, the medicines he would have to give his dear wife were so disagreeable that he preferred someone else should do it.

That was certainly chivalrous of Dr. Herbarius and showed great delicacy of feeling.

What he said when he himself was very ill, and another doctor had been called, does not sound quite so laudable.

When the latter asked him maliciously, why he had called him when he himself had such helpful tinctures, he is said to have answered, "Of course I have them, but I have my private opinions as well, and we two may as well speak frankly with each other. In the case of my beloved wife, I thought, 'do not do unto others as you would not that they do unto you' and in my own case I think, 'what you do unto others, you do not always need do to yourself'. You have no reason to think meanly of me on that account, my remedies are probably much better than yours — no one is sure of anything — but follow my example, and call in someone else, as soon as anything is the matter with you!"

59. I have only three to add to this long list of memorials of places and persons I have made for you, and the first of the three is the house[1]) opposite the bank, which, in old times, belonged to Master Conrad, and is called "Zum Lachenden Wirth". That name originated as follows:

---

1) On the spot where the modern house, Theatinerstrasse 27, now stands.

Ao. 1674 on the ninth of April, a great fire broke out in the Residenz, during the absence of Elector Ferdinand Maria, and great harm was done.

There was great confusion, nobody knowing what to save first, and everybody running about in the scantiest clothing. People hurried out to help them, and almost the first upon the spot was the landlord Martin, nicknamed Homan, who owned the aforesaid house, and was known as a very quiet reserved man, who had the reputation of never having laughed in his life.

The landlord did not think it anything curious when he met Baron Simeoni rushing about in the corridors of the Residenz, in his night-clothes, ringing his hands, and followed by a crowd of ladies-in-waiting and maids, whom he was trying to bring to a place of safety, although he did not know which way to turn, himself. But when he met another group of ladies following the Countess von Waal, sister of the chamberlain of that name, a lady of ripe age and no slender figure, with one side of her hair flying, and no slippers on, and the countess implored him in French to save their lives, the ridiculous side of the scene burst upon him, and he began to laugh for the first time in his life, and the more he tried to stop, the harder he laughed. But at the same time, he seized the good old countess with his left hand, calling out to the others to follow, and with his right arm, he pushed a way for them through the crowds who were rushing to the rescue. In that way he brought them safely to the passage leading to the Theatine monastery, where they found the Electress

Adelheid and her children who had reached the passage, escorted by Marquis d' Harancourt. They were soon joined by Marquis Espinal who had succeeded in rescuing some costly trinkets from the apartements of the Electress, Count von Fürstenberg, who had been quite confused at first, leaving to give orders for the preservation of those parts, which were still standing, which he and the brother of the aforesaid countess, succeeded in saving. Still, a great deal was burned to the ground, namely, the whole side facing the Hofgarten, and beside many valuables of other kinds, a whole series of old portraits of princes was destroyed.

After the fire had raged for a long time, it stopped before the high wall next the bare-footed monks' monastery. It had been caused by a maid-of-honor, who had forgotten to put out her light before going to sleep, and her pillow and bed-hangings had taken fire, and everything was instantly in a blaze.

Noble-minded Adelheid tried to comfort the maid-of-honor, who was in despair over what she had done, and the Elector did the same, when he had been notified of what had happened by three couriers and had reached Munich on the 11th of April.

In regard to the landlord Martin, however, he is said to have rescued and saved a great deal, when he hurried back from the monastery-passage to the fire, whereby he relapsed into his former gravity.

But in the future, when anything was said about the Residenz fire, or the revered Countess von der Waal, his seriousness would forsake him, and he would burst out into a laugh, which shook the walls of the room. No one could listen to it without laughing too, and so his house began to be known as the "Laughing Landlord."

60. Going past the barracks from the Hofgarten gate toward the Englischer Garten, is the place where the so-called "Rockerl" formerly stood. On the spot where the courtyard[1]) of the barracks is, was a little lake with swans upon it, and islands and peninsulars covered with plants, and all sorts of marble vases and bronze figures of human beings and animals. The two metal dogs[2]) in the National Museum were rescued from out the number of those which were smelted down. A group of little hills was upon the site of the barrack building, with tiny edifices, trees and shrubs and in the middle was the so-called "Musenburg" with it's pretty arches and grottoes, in which pillars stood around a Bavaria[3]).

That grotto work was made with tufa, a porous stone, and little shells, in which many-colored stones, red, blue, yellow and all other colors, were mixed; it was the same sort of work one sees in that pretty "Muschelhof" in the old Residenz opposite the Duke Christoph stone.

That sort of work was called Rocaillerie, and the workmen in it, lived in the above-mentioned place, and had their work-shops there, from all of which, the name "Rockerl" developed.

61. The third object I have in mind is a certain tower. You probably think I mean that round tower

1) Now the space in front of the Armee Museum.
2) In the garden, Hof IV.
3) Now on the temple in the Hofgarten.

in Maximilianstrasse, so well-known to debtors, but you are wrong. A picture of the one I mean, is at the beginning of this chapter, namely the old Falken Tower[1]), every trace of which has long since disappeared. The tower went by that name because some of the royal huntsmen and falconers lived in the upper part of the building belonging to it. The tower itself, as everyone knows, was a prison, and the towerkeeper lived on the ground floor of the aforesaid house.

If I were to begin at the beginning, when it was built, at the same time with the neighboring Ludwigs or old Burg, and tell of all those who were imprisoned there up to the last century, the tale would be no short one. So I will only speak of a few, who were privileged at one time or another to take up their abode behind that thick wall.

The Italian knight, Markus Bragadino, called Manulquatro was imprisoned there after he had deceived all manner of people especially the Venetians with his alchemy, and had come to the court of Wilhelm V. at Munich, where his fate overtook him.

Some say he was bound by a gilded rope and led to death, others, that such a rope was suspended from the gallows.

That happened on April 26th 1591.

Another bad customer was the Italian, Fra Solina, of whom you have already heard in connection with Master Conrad of Nürnberg.

A third was the godless young nobleman, Sarazin,

---

1) It stood on Falkenturmstrasse near Maximilianstrasse.

who gave rich Herr Berthold Speirer so much trouble, when the latter came to Munich with money for Duke Johannes, and dismounted at Herr Welser's corner house near Rosenstrasse, in that summer when all crops were in danger, on account of the great heat.

The whole story about Sarazin and Speirer, is in my "Gute Alte Zeit", in the chapter about "The Weather-maker of Frankfort."

I will only say this much here, that Speirer had to pay well for bringing the first weathervane to Munich, because people believed he could make it rain if he wished: but Sarazin had to pay still more dearly. That was Ao. D. 1393.

Then again, three citizens, Triener, Stromer and Haidvokh, were imprisoned there for a short time, during that rebellion, when the power of the dukes was broken for awhile, just as the court-fool had warned them, and were condemned to death for their loyalty, by the heads of the rebellion.

You already know from the story of the Faust Tower that the treacherous burgomaster was thrown into the Falken Tower.

And now, there were three other prisoners of whom I wish to make mention, namely, a highly-respected and aristocratic knight and count, a hot-tempered tailor with his companion, and a lawyer.

The count and knight, Ladislaw von Haag, who was put into Falken Tower, was imprisoned for a still longer time in the tower near the Hofgarten, namely the Christoph Tower, because he had insulted Duke Albrecht V. That was Ao. 1557. He was liberated afterwards, and had many more adventures, especially in Italy where he thought he had won a wealthy bride, while she thought the same thing of him. At last the misunderstanding was cleared up, but not until he had paid so much for expenses and damage-money that he was thankful to reach Germany again. He died Ao. 1567 without heirs, so the earldom became a free Bavarian fief. He lies buried in the church of Kirchdorf, a quarter of an hour from Haag, and his gravestone is there. At first he was buried in a little chapel, about 500 steps from Kirchdorf. But they tore down the chapel and built a small house in it's place and his grave was moved at that time. So Ladislaw went to his own kin, many of the Haags being buried there at Kirchdorf.

The second, the hot-tempered tailor, was named Jörg Hitzberger, and he and his companion Stiler were thrown into the tower because they had been so prominent in the Haag conspiracy Ao. 1596. They were condemned to death, but afterwards to their great relief, were pardoned.

The third, the lawyer, was named Georg Sebastian Plinganser and together with the students, Meindl, Dalmei, Oertel, and especially Hoffmann, organized that group of highlanders, Ao. 1705, who rebelled against the Austrian occupation. The principal reason of the rebellion was that Emperor Joseph I. wanted to raise 12000 Bavarians for Hungary and Italy. Those who were to be sent off, deserted, conspired together, and their number grew to 20000 men, and in a little while it was 40000; then they attacked Burghausen, Schärding, Braunau, and were intending to enter Munich and free it. But the Austrians were warned and the highlanders driven back to Sendling where they met their death. Then the other troops at Vilshofen and Aidenbach were destroyed, and Braunau which was the headquarters of the defence, was delivered over to the Austrians by a certain Ocfort, and so partly by reason of mismanagement, and partly by treachery, the whole rising was put down.

It's leaders were dispersed; Hoffmann was imprisoned and put to death by Austrians, and Plinganser was also taken prisoner; he was brought to Munich for his trial and put into the Falken Tower, from whence he wrote a petition to the Emperor, in the month of June 1706 in which he explained many occurrences and tried to prove that although he had been in the rebellion, he had at the same time hindered much disaster. — A short time after that he was released and later he was government chancellor and counsel at St. Ulrich in Augsburg, where he died Ao. 1737.

In concluding this long chapter, I will add an old rhyme which someone wrote about the Falken Tower.

O sei du frumm und gehorsam fein,
Nur in den Thurm kumm nit hinein,
Ob dich was noch so trutz und wurm,
Ist besser dann im Falkenthurm;
Das kann ich dir für sicher sagn,
Wo du nit glaubst, magst du's beklagn!

(Be good and obedient, lest you get into the tower: However much you are plagued and bothered, it is better than in the Falken Tower. I can give you my word for it, if you do not believe it, so much the worse for you.)

It looks to me as if the author had had personal experience with the tower, he speaks so feelingly!

The Big Wind.

ndoubtedly one of the strangest figures of speech in the Munich dialect is, "Oh yes! at the time of the big wind!" and sometimes "In the year one" is added.

Whoever says that, wants to express a protest, and means in other words, "what you say is no longer possible now-a-days", or, according to the circumstances, "I shall do this or that, under no condition whatever!"

Like many others, I have spent much time in trying to discover what the origin of this "big wind" could have been. But I never reached enough of a conclusion to justify myself in giving it as final. So I will quote the opinions of others, and it is to be hoped that a definite decision will be made sometime.

The first theory which certain wiseacres offer is that the "big wind" means that period when Max

Emanuel was in Brussels as city-commander, and the saying went, was willing to throw away his country of Bavaria piece-meal to the Netherlands, for the sake of a bit of empty glory.

The second theory is quite different. In the middle of the eighteenth century, a new law concerning clothing appeared, because the womenfolk had become so extravagant in caps, skirts, gold-braid and jewelry, that their simple-minded, Christian spouses were at an end of all means and patience.

The law was very welcome to the latter, but their wives would hear nothing of it, although they were warned that they would be stopped on their way to church, or anywhere else, and divested of their caps, gold-braid, and above all, of their jewelry.

So this second theory is that the "big wind" means the hand of justice which swept down upon the more or less fair heads of those obstinate, decked-out women, one Sunday morning, leaving them unadorned, if not penitent for their insubordination.

The third is a confirmation of the second theory, but goes further and mentions a real wind. The police, namely, gained control over the women in part, but not entirely, and some very courageous ones went up the hill to Unser Frauen, the next Sunday, in all their forbidden finery again. The barbarous policemen were on hand once more, but would not have had the victory they did, were it not for a sudden and terrific wind, which raged fearfully, tearing off caps and ribbons, and whisking them over the church and city, as far as the Isar, one cap actually being found on a tree at Ramersdorf. It was due to that atrocious wind, which came like a warning from heaven, that the women conformed to the elector's new law, and the sorrows of the city-police as well as the money anxieties of the husbands were dispersed before it's breath.

A fourth wiseacre adds this. "The high wind which as everyone knows often rages around Unser Frauen, to-day, dates from that other former wind, and is a direct warning from heaven to all women and maidens."

There are only two explanations for the "year one" which is often added to the saying.

Either the beginning of the world is meant jokingly, or the year 1801, when the powers got so much the worst of it with Napoleon, that he compelled them to vacate the left bank of the Rhein and brought such disorder into German possessions, by idemnifying the Rheinish princes at the cost of others, especially by abolishing all clerical states and cities of the empire.

All that change was brought about by decree of the imperial deputation in 1803, according to which the elector of Mayence was the only clerical prince who remained, and he was obliged to move his seat of government to Regensburg, while of 43 imperial cities, 37 lost their independence.

According to that interpretation, the joke is no merry one. But unpleasant as it is, there would be some foundation for it, were it not for the "big wind" which according to all theories dates much further back. And I, for one, am very glad of it, for it would be a pity if the power of that aforesaid conqueror and tyrant had received a memorial from us, in the form of a careless saying.

Now I have given you all the different opinions there are about the "big wind".

I myself, am not satisfied with any of them, however, and still less with what I have been able to find out on my own account. So 1 will leave the subject, until I can say something more definite.

But I hope this much will prove true; that a year 1801 will never return for us Germans, and that the next political "big wind" will not only not harm us, but will waft away any power which is hostile to the German Fatherland.

Sinis.

Now that I am nearing the end of these memories of old Munich, I am sorry that I have not said anything about the coats-of-arms of the different old Munich families, but that would necessitate so many wood-cuts, that I have been obliged to leave them out.

But I wish to mention two more memorials of old Munich, one of which can be seen far and wide in Bavaria, the other being felt throughout Germany.

The first is the two domes on the steeples of Unser Frauen. Many an artist has taken the liberty of making very plain hints about the incongruity of those domes. They do not mean it badly, however.

But the domes' real and dangerous enemies have always been our revered friends, the architects, who are continually proposing taking them away, and putting up spindling, pointed tops, on the good old steeples.

No true Münchener would like that at all, and I doubt if anyone would give a penny toward it. We all know what this so-called improvement means; we have had several experiences of it. Therefore we like the domes just as they are, and prefer them unspeakably to any amount of ornamental iron-work from a modern factory.

And those honest-looking steeples looming up in the distance, seem to say to the traveller, "In this city and country, you can live in peace and security, here your mind will find inspiration and your body comfort."

That has become such an acknowledged fact, that it forms the second token of which I spoke. For from whatever place he comes, when a stranger has once lived here, he cannot tear himself away again.

Judging from that, it seems to me, we must be better off, as regards our way of living and government, than most German countries. I will refrain from comparisons, however, and it would be useless, too, for no Bavarian or Münchener needs me to tell him how well off he is, and the others surely know what the trouble is, at home.

And they are welcome, those others, one and all.

> If he fears the Lord his God,
> And is not overbearing,
> And keeps his word and is clean-minded,
> Rather rough, than affectedly fine,
> Then he is welcome here!

Notes.

Note 1.

"From time immemorial every seventh year, in the carneval season, the coopers have gone through the streets of Munich, dressed in red jackets, black velvet knee-breeches and white stockings, holding barrel-hoops trimmed with green box, in their hands, and preceded by musicians and two clowns. It was a pretty picture, when they stopped before the house of some benefactor or prince, and forming in a wide circle, danced intricate and graceful figures, making arbors and leafy passages with their hoops. Their chief hoop-flinger stood upon a barrel in the middle of the circle, performing tricks, such as flashing a wooden hoop, on the inner side of which three glasses filled with wine rested, over his head and between his legs, without spilling a drop of the wine . . . According to tradition, the Schäffler dance originated at a time of the plague in Munich. A dragon which brought it, had flown down into a well, on the corner of Schrammer and Theatinerstrasse. They held a mirror over the well, and so discovered the dragon, and the source of the poisonous air which issued from the well. The dragon died when it saw its reflection in the mirror and the plague abated. But people still kept their doors and windows closed, and the coopers, to show them that all danger had passed, went dancing through the streets with music. Since that time the well has been known as Spiegelbrunnen. (Mirror fountain.)"   C. A. Regnet.

Note 2.

The following custom is associated with the Fischbrunnen.

"Up to 1878 the butchers of Munich celebrated a ceremony called the "Metzgersprung" (butcher's jump) on carnival Monday, whereby apprentices became assistants. Fourteen days earlier, assistants and apprentices of the trade met in their inn, Zum Kreuzbräu, for the so-called Büschel dance, and it was agreed upon with the head butchers, what should take place on the forthcoming festival, and who should carry the tankard of welcome and the goblet in the procession. Those who were chosen, were called "Hochzeiter" for the time being and were expected to trim the tankards and goblets with flowers, ribbons, and gold and silver cords and tassels.

In the morning all the assistants, clad in holiday clothes, with blue cloaks and fresh flowers on hats and in buttonholes, met in the inn. Then several little sons of head butchers in old Frankish scarlet jackets, black velvet trowsers and green hats, were lifted up onto plump horses, decorated with flowers and ribbons and velvet saddles which the royal stables had furnished. The red-jacketed and white-aproned apprentices, who were to make the jump, mounted horses also, and the procession went first to the "Hochzeiter" then to the old assistants, and then to St. Peter's church where a mass was read for the trade. Those who carried the

15*

tankards and goblets and the old assistant who pronounced the words of the ceremony wore coats trimmed with silver braid, three-cornered hats with the
same, and swords.

From the church, the procession went to the
Residenz where they paid their respects in name of
the trade, and then they went back to their inn. At
noon the apprentices appeared, clad this time in white
from head to foot, with calf-tails hanging all over
them, and followed the old assistant to the Fischbrunnen. They jumped up onto the edge of the
fountain and turned around three times, then a short
dialogue took place between them and the old assistant,
who said he baptised them assistants. Thereupon they
jumped into the water and threw nuts and apples
out among the crowd, who scrambled for them and
were splashed with water by the newly made assistants.

Then they jumped up onto the edge of the fountain again, and fresh white napkins were tied around
their necks, and one of the little sons of head butchers,
decorated them with broad red ribbons, upon which
were thaler pieces.

The Metzgersprung is thought by some to have
originated in the time of a plague, to show the people
that all danger had passed . . ."   C. A. Regnet.

CPSIA information can be obtained at www.ICGtesting.com
Printed in the USA
LVOW03*1513260614

391870LV00013B/382/P